TRANSFORMING WORK

Padmasuri

TRANSFORMING WORK

An Experiment in Right Livelihood

WINDHORSE PUBLICATIONS

Published by Windhorse Publications
11 Park Road
Birmingham
B13 8AB
email: info@windhorsepublications.com
web: www.windhorsepublications.com

Many of the photographs were taken by Roy Marriott
Photo of Kulananda by Dhammarati
Other photos from personal collections
Photo layout Satyadarshin

Cover images (top) courtesy of Windhorse:evolution archives
                (bottom) Digital Vision/Robert Harding
Cover design Sagarapriya
Printed by Interprint Ltd, Marsa, Malta

British Library Cataloguing in Publication Data:
A catalogue record for this book is available from the British Library

ISBN   1 899579 52 4

CONTENTS

About the Author

Padmasuri was born Hilary Blakiston in Aylesbury in 1951. In her mid-twenties, a desire to travel took her to India, a country which was later to become an important part of her life. She moved to Cornwall in 1976 to further her nursing training as a midwife, and came across the Friends of the Western Buddhist Order. Four years later she was ordained within the Western Buddhist Order itself and given the name Padmasuri.

In 1982 she left London, where she had set up a vegetarian restaurant run by a team of Buddhist women, and moved to Pune in India to help establish a medical project among the former Untouchables. Eventually she decided to put her energy into teaching meditation and Buddhism to the former Untouchable Buddhist women. In 1987, on behalf of her teacher, Sangharakshita, Padmasuri helped to conduct the ordination of one of the first women in India to join the Western Buddhist Order.

She returned to England in 1990 and started work in another team-based Right Livelihood business, Windhorse:evolution in Cambridge, where she has worked ever since. The theme of this book is, in part, an exploration of that business.

Acknowledgements

I want to express my gratitude to all the people – far too many to name here – who created Windhorse:evolution from its tiny beginnings back in the late seventies to the business and spiritual community it has become today. Further thanks go to all those who have breathed life into this book either through being interviewed, reading various drafts, editing, or offering wise counsel.

But there is one person I would like to single out for especial thanks and that is Rosemary Tennison, who came in on the project when I had written a first draft but needed some hands-on help. With the creativity of an artist and the sensitivity of a personal tutor, she encouraged me to fill out the material I had gathered into a more comprehensive picture. On seeing that the whole of the Eightfold Path was included within the material (which I hadn't even noticed), she suggested using the eight limbs as a structure. Her professional input has been invaluable, and a lovely friendship developed over the many evenings we spent together talking about work as a spiritual practice. It was a rich period of 'walking the talk' – exemplifying a joint Right Livelihood venture.

'Do well and doubt not.'

Dedicated to my father,
Patrick Blakiston (1914–2003).
He was a true gentleman
loved by many for his unfailing kindness
and motivated by his own search
for life's meaning.
He was a wonderful father to me,
treating my life's choices with
generosity, interest, and respect.
He was looking forward to reading this book
but his life ebbed away
before its publication.
His spirit lives on.

PART ONE

Meaningful Work

INTRODUCTION

THIS IS A BOOK that explores Right Livelihood, the Buddha's teaching on ethical and creative work. This teaching dates back to the time of the Buddha, but what is its relevance and application in today's world? One definition of Right Livelihood is that it is work that deploys our energy wisely, that can give purpose and meaning to our lives, and that is both personally satisfying and of benefit to others.

Men and women are experimenting with ways to use work to transform themselves in many different contexts. I am particularly interested in looking at work that might be called non-vocational, as opposed to types of work that have an overtly altruistic aim, such as nursing or peace-work. My own experience comes from working in a giftware business. This is not a place we may be accustomed to thinking of as a context for spiritual practice, but I will explore how here too we can find opportunities to practise altruism, kindness, mindfulness, and ethics.

There are many books on meditation practice and techniques. The commonest visual representations of the Buddha show him in meditation posture. They can give the impression of lives lived in meditative silence, in calmness, aloof from the world.

Yet most of us are not in a position to meditate 'full-time' or to live apart from the world. We may wish for inner peace and tranquillity, and strive to bring it into our lives, but for most of us this will be in the midst of our working for a living – and that will usually involve a degree of busyness, engagement with the world, exertion, challenge, perhaps boredom, and often stress. My question is, how can we attempt to make 'work' in a materialistic, industrialized society part of our spiritual practice? Can it be our path to wisdom? How can we make it an integral and valued part of our lives, and compatible with our principles?

To answer these questions I draw heavily on my own experience of working for thirteen years in Windhorse:evolution, a Buddhist-run giftware business which started from small beginnings in 1980, when it was called Windhorse Trading. The company later set up retail outlets around the country called Evotion. Today the business in its entirety is called Windhorse: evolution. The purpose of the business is to provide a Buddhist context for team-based Right Livelihood, an exploration of work as spiritual practice. Any profits that are not ploughed back into the business go to fund Buddhist outreach activities around the world. So this book arises from more than a decade within what are still fairly unusual conditions: working full-time in a Buddhist business, run on Buddhist principles, by Buddhists, employing mostly practising Buddhists.

My aim in writing this book is to articulate my knowledge of working in this business. By drawing out common themes I have come upon in these experimental years I hope to offer something of worth to others: ideas and experiences that have a broader application, a relevance to all those interested in creating a holistic life, a context for development within the workplace as well as without.

The book is in three parts. The first goes into the subject of Right Livelihood in general, and how we might practise it in today's complex world, as well as some of the difficulties that may face us as we attempt to put our ideals into practice. The second part of the book explores key areas of transformation, using as a model the Buddha's Noble Eightfold Path, a path that covers all aspects of our being. These aspects or 'limbs' are illustrated with the experiences of various people working in Windhorse:evolution, people dedicated to using the path of work as a tool for transformation. I let these individuals speak for themselves by quoting interviews with them at some length. They speak of their struggles, hopes, and successes – experiences that I hope will find echoes in many people's lives, despite their very different conditions. The third part explores some important themes that are raised by looking at ethical work, such as working in teams, profits, ethical trading, and friendship. Throughout the book, the people within the business describe their experiences and practice at work.

I've always wanted to be able to look back at my life without regrets. Like most of us, I want my life to have meaning, which for me suggests a life in which all its aspects are valued. A key to this has been to ensure that my life is not compartmentalized into 20% of what I like doing and the other 80% that is the rest of my life. My context – my path – has been Buddhism, but in a wider sense it's a search for truth and meaning, for a way to really live.

Although I do not claim to have all the answers, I feel that, together with those with whom I share this endeavour, we have made progress in integrating the many aspects of life: work, spiritual path, friendship, and interests. And a large part of the reason for this has been our collective experience of creative work – or Right Livelihood, the traditional term. For this example and vision I am personally indebted to a number of people – teachers and friends on my path – and through this book I hope to share that experience with others.

1

ATTITUDES TO WORK

I IMAGINE we all want our working years to be a time of creativity. But too often it can feel as if these work years fly by while our hair turns grey, our skin becomes flabby, our children grow up and leave home, and the world revolves at an ever-faster pace. Before we know it we are reaching retirement. By the time retirement comes, some of us may be too old and tired to make good use of our well-earned freedom. We may spend our working lives unengaged, dreaming of a future when we can finally do all the things for which we haven't previously had the time, energy, or money: a future of possibilities that we may or may not live to experience; dreams that can too easily hover on the horizon and take us out of our present experience.

Or do we perhaps consider our real life to take place when we're not working? Evenings, weekends, and holidays around which we work to pay for our lives? This kind of compartmentalizing of our lives can lead us to shut down part of ourselves in order to function at work, suppressing our emotions in favour of being efficient automatons. How much more could we get out of our work and our lives if we could find a broader meaning in what we do, if we could bring the same interest and energy to our jobs that we do to the rest of our lives? Can you imagine having no artificial dividing line between work and life?

These thoughts can seem depressing or they can be a reminder that now is all we know we have, and that we need to find ways to make our present experience matter, whether we are at work or at play, busy or at leisure, alone or with others.

There are compelling reasons for engaging with work as something more than an exchange of labour for money, the most basic being that most of us spend about 40 hours a week at work, for perhaps 40 years of our life, years when we are at our most energetic, creative, active, and focused. To live fulfilling, satisfying lives will surely mean, for most of us, that we must have grappled with the question of how we earn our livelihood, how we fill those 40 hours a week.

Right Livelihood is a term the Buddha used to describe work that is ethical and helpful to one's spiritual development. It is one of the aspects of the Noble Eightfold Path that the Buddha taught as an approach to living an aware and meaningful life – one that could lead the sincere practitioner to liberation. (This Noble Eightfold Path is the basis of Part Two of this book.) The teaching of Right Livelihood has an appeal that is both eternal and universal – as relevant today as it was 2,500 years ago. It is a teaching that is, above all, practical. If put into everyday use it has the power to broaden our awareness, deepen our understanding, and transform our lives.

Perhaps I need to clarify that when I talk about transforming work into a meaningful part of our lives, I mean either our way of earning our livelihood, be it highly or lowly in the world's eyes, or our main occupation, such as parenting, caring for relatives, or voluntary work of some form. Relatively few of us are likely to be pulled towards vocations such as that of doctor, artist, or athlete, so for most of us the meaning in our work will have to come from within. Much of my time at Windhorse:evolution has been spent working on the shop floor, stocking shelves, unpacking boxes, working the till, etc – not at first sight terribly meaningful tasks, and certainly not glamorous, yet the way I have approached them, the friendships I have made, and the vision I have for why I do what I do have added up to a satisfying and meaningful working life for me.

People can find their work unappealing for various reasons. For some it is the career treadmill and lack of like-minded people. Others have jobs in which there is a lack of trust between colleagues which, combined with unhelpful hierarchies, leads to an absence of real communication and mounting frustration with little possibility for change. Others feel a pointlessness of purpose in what they are doing. When life becomes compartmentalized and fragmented and all one's leisure time is spent unwinding, the satisfaction of work can be minimal.

Realistically, the range of choices of work may be limited. Duty to family and other responsibilities, lack of choice due to circumstances, and prejudice can all lead to people having to stay in work that they don't find rewarding. Friends of mine in India – people coming from what were considered the lowest castes and still strongly affected by this conditioning and society's prejudice – have very little choice indeed as to what they do for a living. If they are lucky enough to find work that can support them and their family, they stick with it no matter what the conditions. In various ways, many of us are similarly constrained by the need to support a family. We may feel we have little choice about the kind of work we do, or the context in which we work. Hopefully we will be able to follow the Buddha's guidelines and choose work of an ethical nature. Beyond that, what we can really influence is our attitude to our work. Derrick Bell, an American lawyer and writer, summed this up in his book *Ethical Ambition*.

Millions of Americans – at every income level – find them-selves trapped in unfulfilling jobs. Even in this situation, you will be faced with choices that can have a profound effect on your spirit. If you perform your job as well as you can, treat your co-workers with the respect they deserve, and, if the opportunity arises, stand up in some small way to a practice, policy, or environment that you see as demeaning or simply less than your ideal, your job – even though it may not be the one you always dreamed of – can give you a measure of satis-faction.[1]

I can think of a practical example of this close to hand. A check-out girl at a shop near my home engages with me when I check my groceries through; she seems to see me as a human being, not the thousandth invisible presence behind some cans and vegetables. Her friendliness and responsiveness make my shopping experience more pleasurable. I would imagine it makes her own experience of her work more enjoyable too, be-cause to the extent that we are being truly human, whether in our work or elsewhere, our life has meaning.

This is something open to all of us: to approach our work in the light of our principles, beliefs, and values. In Windhorse: evolution we call it 'work as practice': making our work part of our spiritual life in a variety of ways, from our communication with one another, our attention to our work, even our thoughts. We spend so much time at work. If we can align the time we spend there with our spiritual ideals, it makes sense that we can really start to make progress.

To the extent that we are being truly human, whether in our work or elsewhere, our life has meaning.

In a Buddhist-run business, this alignment is more obvious than in some other workplaces, though it is perfectly possible to sink into a comfortable – or uncomfortable – status quo in a Buddhist-run business, as it is anywhere else. The question remains, however, how open is this approach to people who work in a context set by others? Are the ideas and practices described in this book of any relevance elsewhere? I believe that many of them are. Examining the Buddha's teachings we see an emphasis on the need to look first within, to examine our own ethics, views, thoughts, speech, attitudes. It is always tantalizing to think that if only the external situation were different, then…. There is a Buddhist image that encapsulates this urge: it is like trying to cover the world in leather, rather than make yourself some shoes.² I take this to mean that if we develop our inner resources, we will increasingly be able to deal with whatever external situations throw at us, and less and less will we need the external situations to be 'right'. In working on ourselves we can still have a profound and positive effect on others and on our environment. But the efforts we put into our own personal approach to work will bear fruit whether their outward consequence is immediately felt or not; we will be more human, more alive, and therefore more satisfied, even if our tasks are uninspiring or not explicitly conducive to growth.

A word of caution is perhaps appropriate as this is a difficult area about which to generalize. While we have the power to choose how to work with any given conditions, it's also true that our environment does affect us strongly, be it negative and painful or positive and joyful. Seeking out the conditions that are most conducive to our spiritual growth, if we have that choice, can enable us to transform ourselves more effectively, and perhaps in a more sustainable way. The benefits to be gained from that are not to be lightly discounted.

One of the things that can hold us back from moving to a environment that suits us better is the effect upon us of society's values and expectations. If you are happier sweeping roads than being a secretary, sweep roads! I find I am happier working in a gift shop than being a nurse, though it is a downgrading in the eyes of many. But to be able to be exactly who I am, without pretence, is far more valuable than any external status or praise.

The opposite side of the coin from the feeling that work is meaningless and best over and done with is of course the workaholic. Work becomes all: the only place to find meaning and satisfaction – of a kind. Or the pressure of competition, financial worries, or desire for status can drive us to work longer and longer hours, to the neglect of other aspects of our lives and our development. Achieving a balance is a necessary component of working well; we all need to find perspective in our lives – and there is more to life than work! In this case more attention to our human relationships, our physical well-being, following through other interests and hobbies, or just more contemplative time to explore our inner journey may be needed to redress the balance.

Through my practice of Right Livelihood I have found several ways to widen my perspective within the workplace. Later in the book various people talk about the ways they have approached this issue, such as ethical observance or the practice of mindfulness, how we can take the whole person into account in the workplace, and the effect of having a vision and shared purpose. It may not always work perfectly, but the effort we make is in itself worthwhile. One of the great things about work is that you can see measurable results from it. It's like physical exercise. If you do it you will soon see tangible results.

In the Part Two we'll meet a number of people who recount some of their experiences of Right Livelihood, but we'll start here by meeting Vajradarshini, who describes how she found work as practice to be an effective way of exploring Buddhism. Vajradarshini has been energetically working in teams of Buddhists in Windhorse:evolution shops for more than a decade. She was 21 when she first came across the FWBO. She went along to the Norwich Buddhist Centre to learn meditation 'a bit by chance' and instantly thought 'this is really good'. She learned some basic Buddhist ideas and principles and began reading Buddhist books. However, she didn't know how to use the knowledge she was acquiring. Abstract teachings were not enough; she needed something concrete so that the teaching could translate into a life. 'It's not until I try to apply something that I can believe in it and know it works. Non-applied Buddhism doesn't make sense to me.'

I asked Vajradarshini how she experienced working in a busy shop in Norwich. Most people have the idea of Buddhists as quiet, mindful, leading a simple life with simple work, and doing one thing at a time. How does that align with the hustle and bustle of a busy shop?

'I suppose your question invites another question which is what are "good" conditions for a Buddhist life? If we are able to practise Buddhism in difficult situations, we really learn to practise. In the same way, so-called "good" conditions could just be "easy" conditions; then when the going gets tough we crumble. Perhaps the most difficult thing about our work is that you have to learn to do lots of things at the same time, be a "multi-tasker". There's a Zen story in which Master Seung Sahn is giving a teaching on mindfulness, and he would say, "When you eat, just eat. When you read the newspaper, just read the newspaper. Don't do anything other than what you are doing." One day a student saw him reading the newspaper while he was eating. The student asked if this did not contradict his teaching. Seung Sahn said, "When you eat and read the newspaper, just eat and read the newspaper."

'You can't take things too literally. To work in a shop you've got to learn to multitask. You might be rearranging the soapstone carvings and a stock delivery arrives; there are customers to serve and the phone is ringing. The only way I can marry that situation with attempting to do one thing at a time is by being grounded in myself, emotionally present in all those activities and demands, while not getting lost in them. You get a very strong sense of this at Christmas, our busiest time of year. We are 20 to 30 times busier at this time of year than the rest. I know I'm getting that balance right when, despite the busyness, I feel quite relaxed and at the same time respond and function quickly, and I'm on the ball and don't get stressed. If you get thrown, that's when the difficulties set in. If you can practise mindfulness when serving customers in the run-up to Christmas with some success, that's going to stand you in good stead when practising mindfulness in more ideal conditions.'

During the time she worked in Evolution shops, Vajradarshini was ordained within the Western Buddhist Order and given her name, which means 'diamond vision' or 'she who sees reality'. I asked her if she could possibly sum up her experience of that time.

'Teams of people, that's my practice. The total is more than the sum of the parts: together you can do so much more than you can separately. I have an antisocial side too. Sometimes it seems like hard work having to consider so many other people, and I would rather just potter in the garden shed alone. But mostly I love projects, bringing people together, and I love to work. Work as a practice, for me, is far more tangible, than my meditation practice.

'We all have habits in the form of patterns, and these patterns are like what they call fractals. Take the example of a cauliflower: it's a fractal, albeit imperfect. If you break off a piece of a cauliflower, that piece looks like a small cauliflower, and if you break a bit off that piece, that too is the same shape as the cauliflower. It is as if the large cauliflower is made up of tinier and tinier cauliflowers. We too are like that. Our little habits may also be a reflection of major trends in our life. We can recognize and chip away at our little habits. One of mine is not finishing things. We can work on and change these habits, and in doing so start also to work on the major trends and begin to change the whole direction of our lives. This is part of how I see work as my practice.'

One thing I treasure about Buddhism is that the Buddha did not encourage blind beliefs or expect people to take his teachings on trust. Instead he urged people to reflect on his teachings and try them out in order to see the outcome for themselves, encouraging them to test out his guidance, as a goldsmith tests gold in the heat of a fire.[3] In a sense, that is what I feel I have been doing in the process of writing this book: gradually becoming convinced that Windhorse:evolution can be a path of total transformation through asking questions of people like Vajradarshini, airing doubts, and challenging speculations. It is in this fire of experience that we become convinced of the benefits in the teaching of Right Livelihood.

2

FINDING MY PATH

WORK HAS ALWAYS BEEN a significant part of my life. I have been lucky. Apart from a few months' temping, work has never been something I have done purely to earn a wage. For my life to be meaningful, I needed to feel engaged and happy with my work, for I have not wanted to work while inwardly brooding over some imagined future that may never happen. I have also been fortunate enough to be able to organize my life so that work and the rest of my life have not been separate strands with little linkage between them. Instead there has been coherence between the two. I doubt I shall depart from this life wishing I had chosen a different way to spend so many of my precious years. Nowadays work holds an importance for me as significant as my meditation practice, my friendships, my family, holidays, and retreats. I see myself as striving, with others, to create a better world.

In my twenties I took up nursing training, for two reasons: it seemed a useful way to play my part in alleviating suffering, and I had a reawakened desire to work in the third world. A three-year nursing course, followed by further midwifery training, constituted a passport to that world, though I still rejected the concepts of career or vocation. It was only after qualifying as a nurse that I came across Buddhism, which became more and more the focus of my life.

As a Buddhist I have looked for ways to bring my working life into line with my values – not just in its content, but in my approach – for example, how to develop positive mental states and greater awareness. As I became more and more involved with Buddhism, I looked for a seamless way of life, one in which I could 'work' at being myself, at being truly human, wherever I found myself. This led me to make some quite radical changes in my life, which I was fortunately able to do as I had no other major commitments and a context into which I could throw myself.

When I was a fledgling Buddhist, back in the late seventies, Buddhist business ventures were, as far as I know, just coming into existence in the West. There was a lot of enthusiasm, a pioneering spirit, much experimentation, but very little expertise. Rather like Plato's famous dream of a society based on justice, *The Republic*, others too had a dream. One of the first dreamers, in the early 1970s, was Sangharakshita, an Englishman and founder of a worldwide Buddhist organization called the Friends of the Western Buddhist Order (FWBO). His dream was that this community of Buddhists, or *sangha*, would address all aspects of life: social life, the home, and economic livelihood. This would comprise, firstly, public centres where meditation and Buddhism could be taught together with more indirect methods of self-transformation such as yoga and the arts; secondly, living communally with other Buddhists; and thirdly, collective work.

Buddhist practice is often spoken of as a transformation of self, yet Sangharakshita also saw how it could mean the transformation of a whole society. He considered that if a number of active, alert, and inspired individuals could work together in a dedicated fashion, they could have a huge influence on whole groups of people. We could become new societies in miniature, within the old.

This blueprint excited many of us. We wanted not just to hear about the dream, or even dream the dream, we wanted to live the dream – so we threw ourselves into his vision with gusto. Sangharakshita is both practical and pragmatic. In the early days of the FWBO people would finish a week-long retreat on which they had been learning about Buddhism in a conducive environment and not want to return to their workplace or living situation. They knew how easy it was to become submerged in worldly pursuits, which for many contrasted starkly with the positive conditions of the retreat. It was out of this build-up of frustration and idealism that residential communities arose, the first public centres already having got under way. Collective Right Livelihood ventures were the slowest to take off, and the most difficult to sustain, yet there were a number of dedicated people who were happy to give them a go, at least for a while.

I was 27 years old in 1978, and had moved from being a mid-wife in Cornwall, via living in a Buddhist retreat centre for women in Norfolk, to find myself in Bethnal Green in London's East End, living in a community with six other Buddhist women. In December of that year, I was keen to be involved in the public opening of the London Buddhist Centre, then the biggest FWBO centre in the UK. I wanted to be in on the action, because I was a dreamer too. For a number of months I worked part-time at a local hospital to earn my living, but my heart was elsewhere. My foremost engagement with life was a few hundred yards down the road from the disinfectant-smelling wards, at the incense-perfumed shrine-room, sitting at the feet of a massive golden Buddha image.

I then gave up nursing to manage the Cherry Orchard, a Buddhist-run vegetarian restaurant that still thrives today. I threw myself into it with a group of women friends with all our inexperience and naïve yet imaginative dreaming. We had no clear vision of where we were trying to go, but we had a lot of fun in the kitchen, and deep friendships were forged, many of which continue to this day. This snapshot skims over a period that was, in reality, very hard for those working in some of those early businesses – long hours, a basic standard of living, and, most importantly, not always a clear vision. Were we really transforming anything merely by keeping ourselves afloat, dropping out of society a little, and maintaining a certain inward-looking cosiness? Doubts were creeping in.

At this point, I left the restaurant to follow another dream, that of living and working in India. I was to work as a nurse and teacher as part of the extraordinary 'revolution' taking place there within the former untouchable community and the mass conversions to Buddhism, bringing Buddhism alive once again in the country of its birth. But that is another story.[4]

It was on my return to England nine years later that my involvement with Windhorse:evolution began. I was looking for a new project to devote myself to, and they were keen to open a gift shop in Cambridge, where they were based. I had moved to Cambridge and was looking at what I might do next. Along with some other Buddhist women who were looking to work collectively, I was asked whether I would be interested in helping to run this shop. Although some of the others were keen, I was not. I argued that selling gifts encouraged greed, and that it was neither something I wholly approved of, nor something I wanted to do.

Well, Windhorse galloped ahead and suitable premises were found. I was asked whether I would consider being involved in the first months of running a shop, as all the other women were new to Buddhism and had no experience of team-based Right Livelihood. A little reluctantly, I said I would work there part-

time for a while. I went into this somewhat unwillingly, unrec-
onciled to the selling of giftware. I imagined working there a
few months and then returning to part-time nursing to support
myself until I found something I really wanted to do.

I was astonished that after a very few weeks I found myself
not only enjoying the work but also engaging in the team spirit,
interacting in conversations with interesting and interested
customers, and even liking some of the goods we sold. It was
particularly pleasing to observe a happy customer walking out
of the shop with a present for a friend. In spite of my previous
attitudes towards money, I was excited at the profits we were
making available to give away. What was more, other women
were attracted to move to Cambridge and involve themselves in
the endeavour. I was gradually becoming convinced again of
the value of team-based Right Livelihood as a concrete and
direct way for people to broaden their experience and deepen
their understanding of Buddhism, even if it was in the guise of a
gift shop. It began to dawn on me that what was happening was
not as divorced from the revival of Buddhism in India as I had
thought.

March 2001 marked the tenth birthday of Cambridge's Evolution shop. Apart from doing a three-month solitary retreat in
New Zealand, I have worked (or played) in the shop all that
time. I had previously done a lot of jobs that from the outside
might seem far more interesting than selling picture frames,
candles, nodding velour dogs, and cushion covers to the general public. However, more satisfaction has come from being
with Buddhists working together, who are interested in mutual
spiritual development, and creating money to give away for
spreading the Dharma, the Buddha's teaching.

During this decade many women, from all over the world,
have spent a number of years giving their time, energy, and creativity to the growth of Evolution Cambridge, at the same time

gaining inspiration and enjoyment. Many have also gone through periods of personal struggle, which seems to be part of the growing pains of leading a spiritual life. A book of photographs reminds me of all those individuals. Some women have stayed for just a couple of years, others four or five years, each adding their own characteristic expertise and inspiration. Some have moved on to different parts of the business. Of those who have left, most have been grateful for the opportunities it provided for developing friendliness and friendships, and for experiencing their potential beyond just the nature of the task. They left with a far stronger sense of Buddhism in action in the modern world. There have also been some who haven't found the structures of such a full-on life helpful or suitable for them.

By choice, though not always an unequivocal one, I never got the husband, children, house, or garden I had envisaged as a teenager. I have spent many of the last twenty-five years living in Buddhist communities with other women, though I now live simply and alone in an adequate one-bedroomed flat, tending a postage stamp of a garden. I have a livelihood that is meaningful, and an intelligent and warm network of friends who are a great source of inspiration to me, including a long-standing lover. I don't consider my work colleagues to be merely associates; they are friends with whom I am sharing a great deal of my life. For most of my working life I have put myself in a communal endeavour where I can deepen my friendships with others who aspire to the same ideals, enabling my work to be part of my aspiration in life.

Because of them, and the money we make to give away, I am happy to commit myself for the foreseeable future to this big experiment in team-based Right Livelihood. I continue to work in various capacities within Windhorse:evolution, working in the shop, befriending people in the business, and making forays into overseas buying. I am also part of the management team.

Now I am working on this book. My life today is as meaningful as it has ever been. And, incidentally, I have decided that living to the full is my career.

My experience, as you will see, is echoed by many others who have participated in this venture who wanted to find an effective way to practise spiritually and to whom work seemed a good medium for that practice. Let us now turn to examine in a bit more depth this twenty-first-century western Buddhist business and how it came about.

3

SETTING UP THE BUSINESS

WALK THROUGH THE DOORS of Windhorse:evolution's main office in the suburbs of Cambridge and at first you will not notice anything different from any other such company. From the outside, the warehouse and offices look like any of the other industrial units on the estate: a few cars and vans are parked in the yard outside, while a 40-foot container truck is being unloaded of its boxes with foreign labels. Now move inside the warehouse and watch the boxes move down the conveyor belt into the further reaches of the warehouse and look at the gaggle of young men standing ready to catch them at the other end and stack them up. Some of them are white-skinned and well-spoken, others have regional accents, and they are all mingling easily with men of varying shades of swarthier complexion. They look quite energetic, and though they mostly work in silence you may overhear words of Spanish, Hindi, or German, and you will certainly hear Aussie and American twangs. Some of them have shaven heads, others ponytails; one has dreadlocks, several just have neat short-back-and-sides. There is no chart music playing, no music at all.

Look around the warehouse, which is as big as a football pitch, and you will see rows of similar boxes piled up to the ceiling on metal racking. A few of the boxes are open to reveal a variety of items, from wooden Balinese masks to packets of sequinned purses bulging out of polythene bags and smelling of Indian incense. However, if you raise your gaze to the end of the warehouse, beyond the boxes of artefacts, you will see something rather unexpected – unless, of course, you are in the know: a massive and utterly serene Buddha figure, seated in meditation, painted in blue and gold on the breeze block wall, as though keeping watch over the corridors of stock. The whole warehouse is perfumed with the scent of sandalwood.

Push open a door to the open-plan offices and you will find other men looking at computer screens, answering telephones, poring over spreadsheets, or highlighting stock-lists with felt-tip pens. It is no different from any similar office, but now take a look at the desks. There are pot plants and vases of flowers and exquisite reproductions of Tibetan thangkas and Buddha images. On some, there are photographs of Sangharakshita, and many have smiling photographs of friends. It is not altogether a tidy office, the decor and aesthetics do not speak of cut-throat business or even great efficiency, but it feels friendly, and it is quiet and concentrated. You might enquire where the managing director's office is situated and be surprised to find he is in a corner of the general office, talking on the phone at his slightly shabby 1950s desk, his laptop computer open before him. Around his feet lies an array of stock samples. If you wander further afield, you will discover other open-plan offices with teams of men or women busily working away, each different but all with the same flavour. You will notice many shrines in discrete corners or atop filing cabinets. You will also pass a few much larger shrines displaying grand Buddha images, flowers, half-burned candles, and incense in bowls. The shrines have been set up on wooden pallets covered with brightly-coloured cloths, with meditation cushions in front of them.

If it happens to be lunchtime, you might encounter a couple of men strumming guitars or a young woman practising her cello, while others play table tennis. Some are going out for walks, mostly in twos, or sitting in the car park cradling steaming cups of tea. Stop for a moment and read the noticeboard: 'Lunch time concert in the music room in aid of the Karuna Trust', 'Marichi from the accounts team will give a talk on Renaissance art', 'Volunteers needed to help create the shrine for our next full-moon celebration.' And if you see a list of names of those who want a lift to Birmingham for FWBO Day celebrations, not only will you see the names of people such as John, Maria, Paul, and Eve, but also Sanskrit and Pali names such as Lalitavajra, Vijayamala, Keturaja, and Dhirangama.

What is it that distinguishes Windhorse:evolution from other companies trading in giftware? Most significantly, of course, the business is Buddhist and centred on the spiritual development of all those who work there. It has developed as a team-based Right Livelihood experiment, with teams of men or women working together. It was initially set up in order to provide an environment in which members of the Friends of the Western Buddhist Order can live and work together to practise Right Livelihood as taught by the Buddha. From its humble origins as a market stall it has grown to include about 200 full-time workers, as well as a number of volunteers and part-time workers, the latter helping mainly in retail outlets across the country.

Another distinguishing characteristic of Windhorse:evolution is that it gives away much of its profits. In 2000 the business had a turnover of £9.8m, a growth of 9% on the previous year. It made a profit of £1.2m of which half was ploughed back into the business and half was given away to finance various activities and capital projects run by the FWBO. There are about sixty

FWBO Buddhist centres in towns across the UK and Europe, Australasia, India, and North and South America, many of which have been helped by donations from the business. Windhorse:evolution comprises a 82,000 sq.ft. warehouse and central offices in Cambridge, and seventeen Evolution shops, mainly in the UK, but also in Valencia (Spain), Essen (Germany), and Dublin (Eire). The shops vary in size and have a turnover of between £515,000 in our largest shop to £197,000 in the smallest. The majority of the people who work in the business are Buddhist, many living in residential spiritual communities.

In remunerative terms, the business operates on a principle of 'give what you can, take what you need.' None of us receives a salary as such. We have our basic needs, such as rent and food, paid for, with a small amount of money on top. Vajraketu, as managing director, receives the same pay as a 20-year-old with no qualifications, no work experience, and who is new to Buddhism. Retreats in the countryside, either with groups of other Buddhists or in solitude, are considered an important part of the spiritual life, so six weeks of retreat are provided each year, together with a number of weekend retreats. This sustains a lifestyle that values simplicity and contentment rather than the acquisition of material possessions.

Of course, not everyone is able to live at this basic rate, particularly those bringing up families. Someone who is supporting children will receive considerably more money than the managing director, even if he or she 'only' does manual work. But the underlying principle is the same: having one's needs met and not amassing personal wealth. Some people formerly worked in well-paid jobs and have accumulated savings, while others have inherited money. It is entirely up to them whether to take the basic pay or live off some of their previous earnings. In this sense we do not run on a completely common purse, and there is no suggestion that anyone should give their money away.

The various statistics on the present-day business presented here are impressive, I believe, in their own right. But they are quite staggering when you look at the small and unprofessional beginnings and its gradual, lurching unfolding. The rest of this chapter is therefore an outline of its history from a front room in a run-down house in the early 1980s, where a handful of Buddhists were selling a few gift items and making no profit, to the multi-million pound business that it is today.

Windhorse Trading, which is still its legal name, was started in 1980 by two Buddhists who ran market stalls in trendy Camden Lock and Covent Garden, buying small items such as mobiles, Chinese fans, durries, and jewellery from local wholesalers. A rather scruffy shop in Bethnal Green, close to the London Buddhist Centre, served as their base. They also exhibited their goods at trade shows, and were well pleased with sales of around £3,000 from their first show, though sadly they had neither the back-up stock nor any spare money to buy the goods, so some orders had to be cancelled. To begin with, the business just did not have the financial backing to get off the ground.

Undaunted, they soldiered on and others came to help. With borrowed money, they leased a Volkswagen van and drove around the country selling to small gift shops. After a few years, they stopped the market stalls and concentrated on wholesaling, but it was incredibly hard. Cash flow was a constant problem. In the first year they had no money and had lost everything. They borrowed money from trusting friends, and slowly traded their way out of difficulties. But for the first ten years it was hard to keep the business solvent, and a lot of time and energy was spent juggling with money. The Windhorse philosophy for that period was 'grow until there ceases to be a problem'. It was ten years of financial worry.

Vajraketu, today's managing director, takes up the story here. He had been was asked to go to London because the business had hit a difficult patch. He was at a bit of a loose end because his planned return to India, where he had been teaching Buddhism, had fallen through because of visa restrictions. 'I found Kulananda (one of the founders) horribly overstretched. It seemed to me that he needed two people to assist, one to help with the business per se and the other to focus on personnel. There were about eight people in the business at the time. I remember one person worked alone in the warehouse every day, which was really just a small storeroom, and he also had to cook lunch for everyone. It was not very conducive to teamwork. Everybody else worked in offices upstairs. Today over thirty men work in the warehouse alone.

'The notion of working in Windhorse seemed far less glamorous than teaching the Dharma. I remember when I first came back from India and did a tour around UK FWBO centres speaking about our work in India, I got a lot of positive feedback. People would say how much they admired what I was doing. It was very gratifying. But I recall talking to Kulananda and saying that I thought he needed a lot more commitment to do what he was doing. Kulananda was working very hard trying to realize the vision of making money for the FWBO, whereas in India I got an immediate "hit" teaching Buddhism. It seemed ironic to me that people would respond and look up to me more for what I was doing than what he was doing. Once I realized I couldn't return to India, America was suggested to me, and that too seemed rather glamorous. So when subsequently I was asked to go to Windhorse, which was in a run-down building in a grotty area of East London with boxes of inflatable parrots, and Pierre Cardin scented notepaper....'

I asked Vajraketu why he thought Sangharakshita had thought it more important to help out in Windhorse than run a retreat centre in America.

'I don't know, I can only speculate. Because Kulananda was under strain and had little support, if nothing dramatic happened he was going to close the business. The most exciting answer to your question would be that Sangharakshita's vision was so broad that he felt Right Livelihood would play an important part in the FWBO of the future; if it closed it would be a body blow to that. Also he was a good friend of Kulananda so it might have been influenced by his desire to support him.'

So Vajraketu and his friend Ruchiraketu arrived in 1985 at the not very glamorous Windhorse offices. As Vajraketu says, 'There was little sense of community among people when I got there, and being undermanned the amount of work to be done was enormous, both in the business and in the community.'

One of his first tasks to go looking for new premises outside London. They decided to move to Cambridge because it was close enough to London, where they had already built up business connections, and it was a town where the FWBO wasn't yet established. They anticipated another FWBO Buddhism and meditation centre would be set up in the town as well as the business.

It was extraordinary how the move to Cambridge worked out. First they managed to find a house to rent in Newmarket Road. Then, just by chance conversations or connections, they ended up renting a small, inexpensive warehouse that was due to be demolished within three years just fifty metres away from the community. Subsequently, other properties almost fell into their laps, all within a stone's throw of one another, and now this small pocket of Cambridge is sometimes referred to as the Buddhist village.

'It was only years later that I realized how fortunate we were. In the beginning we had no money and could barely afford the deposit on the house. How we managed to get references for the warehouse I can't imagine, for we were still losing money. I was working away at stabilizing the personnel and general morale, and the spirit was improving, but the business was still suffering.'

In February 1986, Windhorse had a bit of a breakthrough, which was to be the beginning of a turnaround. They showed their merchandise at a trade show and in five days they took orders totalling only £8,000, which reflected their lack of stock. Even the stock they had was tired-looking, because they had no money to buy any more. But then a buyer from W.H. Smith came to their stand. Vajraketu continues the story.

'Kuladitya made very good contact with her. He was about 25 at the time and had blond curly hair, which may have had something to do with it, but as a result we got an order from them for 40,000 of one particular item – a palm tree desk organizer selling at 80p each. It was a huge order, but we had no money to buy such a quantity from Taiwan, and the bank wouldn't lend us money because we didn't look strong. It was a friend called Allan Hilder who lent us the money to buy the goods. Allan ran a lighting business and was energetic, resourceful, and intelligent. We often ended up on adjacent trade show stands, so we befriended each other. I think he adopted us as a bit of a pet project and was amused at how clueless we were! He lent us £17,000, which he thought was no big deal, on the grounds that we sold to W.H. Smith for £30,000. We did so, and made a profit of £13,000. The previous year we'd lost £11,000 so that was a lot of money to us!'

The business was undercapitalized, partly because imported gifts and handicrafts have to be paid for three months before they arrive in the country, and then there is another month or two before our customers pay us. Financing the gap at that stage in the business was very difficult. We had to put an enormous amount of energy into borrowing money. There was a very helpful fringe banker, David Robertson, who used to lend money when nobody else would. Most of our customers were small shopkeepers who would come into contact with us through trade shows. Subsequently the goods would be sold from 'cash and carry'-style vans, one of the van salesmen visiting these customers at regular intervals.

At the beginning of 1987, Kulananda was still the driving force of the business as well as the buyer, obtaining stock both from UK wholesalers and buying direct from Taiwan. Vajraketu was doing most of the administration and finance, while Ruchiraketu was looking after the spiritual welfare of those in the business. Vajraketu describes those times.

'Kulananda was somewhat worn out and under a huge strain. He'd established the business, but it had been a slog, and the business was identified with him. I found it difficult to engage with it. In some respects it was Kulananda's baby. Myself, along with two others who were newly ordained, wanted to run it on our own and talked with Kulananda. He was more than happy to pass it on, and also wanted to establish Buddhist activities in Cambridge, which is exactly what he did. So he went off on a long solitary retreat and on return became chairman of the newly-established Cambridge Buddhist Centre, while I became the managing director of the business, and also started doing the buying.

'I'd only done one overseas buying trip with Kulananda before he left the business, during which time we stopped off in Tokyo to get ideas for products. This was another stroke of luck: I bought a desk calendar with magnets on it. Back in England, I showed it to a designer and inspired by the original product he made something different. Kulananda and I took the new product to W.H. Smith and they immediately bought 10,000 pieces. I was so chuffed! The next few years were still quite a struggle, although the business was in better shape. We were constantly short of money, because there was fast growth. We were going to more trade shows, there were more sales and more vans selling to gift shops around the country. A whole rolling momentum got going. It's almost a mathematical truth that when you're growing a business fast you need capital; if sales are growing you need much more stock; therefore most energy is going into finding and borrowing money, and apologizing to people we couldn't pay. My sleep and meditations were dominated by money, or rather the absence of it!'

However, Windhorse slowly began to make a profit, although it was a long time before we saw any cash. If you develop a business very quickly you hope eventually to get to a point where you are big enough to generate large profits. This way of growing was Kulananda's vision. Vajraketu just took it on without thinking about it one way or another.

'We started borrowing what seemed at the time unimaginably large sums of money, on the assumption that when we had to pay them back they wouldn't be unimaginable any more. That was the case and we were vindicated by it. I remember a time when we owed £700,000, which was seven times what the business was worth, whereas £700,000 is now less than a quarter of what it is worth.'

It was in 1988 that the seeds of the Evolution shops were planted, almost – it seems – by a fortuitous accident.

'I'd bought too much stock and sales were rather flat. One day I noticed a big empty shop in Cambridge and discovered it was owned by Magdalene College. On a bit of a whim, I wrote to the college bursar and offered him £2,000 for a temporary Christmas-time lease, explaining that we were a charity. Amazingly we got the lease. So now we had this huge shop that like so many other things seemed just to fall into our lap. We did a good job of making an empty shop look quite interesting without spending much money on it. It was a big success. We displayed the merchandise on towers of breezeblocks with glass on top and it looked kind of trendy. This was the start of the Christmas shops, which were brilliantly suited to the FWBO culture, for there were lots of Buddhist centres around the country which needed money, and they had people involved in them who were ready to work for short periods of time to make money for them.'

For about six years, Windhorse had these temporary shops run by FWBO centres involving all sorts of people and proving very profitable. This was a time when interest rates were high and the country was in recession, so it was easy to pick up short leases because there were lots of empty shops. People would enjoy the experience of team-based Right Livelihood, but when the shops closed they would think, what now? This led to permanent Evolution shops. You could say that the Evolution chain started by accident because it was over-stocked.

In 1989 the business moved from the small warehouse 'down the road' to larger premises in Fulbourn, a village some five miles away.

'It's a bit of an indication of how the business has grown that what we've done is respond to opportunities when we've seen them rather than working to a plan. My vision of "long term" at that time was only six months ahead.'

By 1993 the head office and warehouses had to move once again to bigger premises, and we found a good site on an industrial estate back in Cambridge, the one described at the beginning of this chapter. By this time the business was really starting to make profits they could give away.

'It was a big thing for me. Prior to that we had only managed to give away a little to India, and to the office of the Western Buddhist Order in England to run its administration – between £5,000 and £10,000 a year – and we'd made a one-off donation towards starting a retreat centre in Spain. Sangharakshita has suggested where the profits could go, over the amounts given to local Buddhist centres in towns where there are Evolution shops. We decided to pass on to him the responsibility of where all the profits should go. We felt he had more of an overview of the FWBO as a whole and where the money might be used best. We didn't want to carry the burden of that responsibility ourselves. The first big project we funded, to the tune of £45,000, was the purchase of land in Bodh Gaya, the site of the Buddha's Enlightenment in India. From then on we were able to give away substantial amounts of money, which was very satisfying.

> **There can be a certain tension between running a successful business and promoting the spiritual welfare of those involved in it.**

'Historically, as a business, not much has changed since then, only growth. We source and buy products from more countries. There is more product diversity. I wanted to improve the quality and aesthetics so in the 1990s I was diversifying our supply chain. However, it is not always plain sailing, even now.

'There can be a certain tension between running a successful business and promoting the spiritual welfare of those involved in it. We did have some problems related to this three or four years ago. We had grown very rapidly for several years and towards the end of that period we became over-stretched. Those most committed to the business were fully occupied running the business side of things, and the spiritual side perhaps got a bit neglected. We were taking on a lot of new people because we needed to get the work done, not because we consciously wanted to expand the number living and working with us.

'We made several errors at this time, mainly in terms of not being sufficiently attentive and sensitive to some people. Although it was not our intention to do this, the business started to take priority over people's needs. A few things happened then that I regret. For example, there was one young chap who was keen to take on more responsibility. We were happy to pile it on him as he was so willing, but we did not stop to consider if we were asking too much of him, and crucially we did nothing to give him extra help and support to enable him to ease into his new responsibilities. In the end he got overwhelmed and had to leave, and he was bit undermined by it all. He felt he had failed, though really we had failed him. So we decided to stop growing until we were more confident in our ability to handle the growth without losing sight of why we were doing it. It's a sad irony that our most profitable year came during this period when we to some extent lost sight of our broader spiritual goals.'

As Vajraketu's reminiscences have shown, this period of development was not without its difficulties. The business was growing rapidly, new people were joining, and the existing team, stretched in all areas, found it increasingly difficult to pass on the spirit of the business to newcomers. Many who joined the business at that time didn't see why we did things the way we did and, quite understandably, they had issues with that. Consequently, a period of consolidation followed, when growth was controlled – but maintaining a balance between the growth of the business and the spiritual needs of the people within it needs constant attention. Business needs can be immediate and obvious. Developing work as a spiritual practice can be subtler and less immediately apparent. However, the fact that it is difficult, and can and will go wrong at times, shouldn't detract from the fact that it is possible to have both a successful business and a context in which people can effectively practise and develop. Windhorse:evolution is one such experiment.

PART TWO

The Noble Eightfold Path

INTRODUCTION

WE SAW IN CHAPTER 1 that Right Livelihood is one of the stages of the Noble Eightfold Path taught by the Buddha. This is probably the most widely-known formulation of the Buddha's teaching, and dates back to the first discourse after his Enlightenment. The teaching is as appropriate for, and applicable to, us in the twenty-first century world as it was in ancient India. The Buddha's vision at the time of his Enlightenment had a lasting effect on him, and it informed the rest of his life and teaching. His vision and its implication still reach out and touch us profoundly today.

The Buddha noticed that all human beings experience both joy and suffering. He saw how we get old, become sick, and die. Despite these realities, he recognized that some people lead lives rich in meaning and purpose, while others drift directionless with no aspirations. Of these, some experience so much discontent that they become bitter and gnarled, even destructive.

So what were his vision and his teaching? Put succinctly, he saw the truth of change. On both the material and spiritual plane, he saw that everything was in process. He saw clearly that things arise and then pass away. More than that, he realized that whatever arises does so in dependence on conditions, and whatever ceases does so because those conditions cease. He understood therefore that change does not happen by chance. What the Buddha saw at the time of his Enlightenment was a vision of the human predicament, an understanding of human existence itself.

He saw that life contains unsatisfactoriness, disharmony, and suffering. From this raw comprehension, he saw the truth of the causes of suffering: how we are driven by a selfish thirst to appropriate things and people, or conversely to push them away so as to boost our sense of self. This paints a rather bleak picture, but luckily he did not stop there. He went on to see the truth of the total eradication of suffering, synonymous with an awakened state of being: Enlightenment itself. Lastly, he realized the truth of the way leading to the cessation of suffering, which he formulated as the Noble Eightfold Path. This understanding of suffering, its causes, its cessation, and the path leading to the cessation of suffering, are what have come to be called the Four Noble Truths.

> What the Buddha saw at the time of his Enlightenment was a vision of the human predicament, an understanding of human existence itself.

To look in detail at why we suffer when we try to appropriate things or push them away would be a book itself. Briefly, it is because all things are subject to change, to decay, and eventually to death or dissolution, so that those things we want to be close to, or to own, are unreliable – we lose them or they are subject to change. Conversely, when it is something we *don't* like, we suffer when we are in contact with them. The Noble Eightfold Path is like a gradual training process that helps us to see this truth more and more clearly and gradually to transform our understanding and our experience. The process starts at any point; we can slowly build on whatever state we find ourselves in.

The Noble Eightfold Path, the fourth of the Four Noble Truths, is the gradual path that can liberate us from suffering; it covers all aspects of our lives. The initial glimmers of truth that we all experience from time to time are Right Vision and they can encourage us to take up the path of transformation. We start by engaging our emotions in that transformation through Right Emotion. Right Speech provides principles about truthful, kindly, and harmonious speech, and this is followed by Right Action which involves cultivating ethical observance. Right Livelihood involves bringing our practice into how we make our living. The Buddha goes on to point out the importance of making conscious effort in the way we lead our lives through Right Effort, and to the need for awareness of things, ourselves, others, and reality through Right Awareness. Finally, he exhorts us to develop higher states of consciousness by Right Concentration or 'samma samadhi'. Individually and collectively these eight limbs reveal a realm of expansive possibilities that encourage us to live our lives more fully and with meaning.

It was a great joy and inspiration to realize, as I became immersed in this book, that all the limbs of the Noble Eightfold Path are included within it, for it has always been a nagging question at the back of my mind whether the experiment of team-based Right Livelihood, the way we are doing it in Windhorse:evolution, can really be a *total* path of transformation. If the way we work is to be a full expression of a Buddhist way of life that helps us to develop more enlightened states of being, it must have all the limbs of the path within it. It is this complete approach to the spiritual life, these eight stages, seen through the lens of a working life, that I present in this section.

Through writing this book, I came to realize that I had come across the Buddha's teaching as he explained things to

Subhadda, his last disciple, in the *Mahāparinibbāna Sutta* (*Dīgha Nikāya* 16). Subhaddha has a conundrum that he puts to the Buddha. He says there are many religious teachers who have orders and followings, naming a few individuals who were popularly regarded as saints. He is puzzled as to which, if any, have realized the truth. The Buddha replies, 'Never mind whether all, or none, or some of them have realized the truth. In whatever religion, philosophy, or discipline the Noble Eightfold Path is not found, no practitioner will be found having attained irreversible higher states of consciousness. On the other hand, truth seekers can be found having attained irreversible higher states of consciousness that will have a substantial effect on the world wherever the Noble Eightfold Path is found.' The Buddha goes on to say how the Noble Eightfold Path is found in his teaching, and among those who follow it sincerely are to be found Enlightened men and women.

Those who have attained Enlightenment do so as a result of certain conditions which come from following the Noble Eightfold Path – although it may not be conceptually formulated as such in their minds. In the next eight chapters we shall be looking at each of these limbs in turn, with the help of stories from some of those working in Windhorse:evolution. The conditions they enjoy – though by no means perfect, and though they do not work for everyone – are 'good enough', if the right kind of effort is applied. Though I would be unable to claim that there are Enlightened men and women working here, I can say with certainty that there is no reason why, if we keep practising, there might not be one day. That is when the eight limbs of the Path reach perfection, and it is to the first of these, Right Vision, that we now turn.

4

FACING THE TRUTH: RIGHT VISION

BY WHAT DO WE GUIDE our life? Is it inherited beliefs and values, the mores of society, a flash of insight that moved or changed us, or perhaps the lessons of life as we grow older and hopefully wiser? We all have some values and beliefs that guide our choices and shape our lives – ideas and ideals that lie within us, but which may be more or less conscious. The Buddha encourages us both to make these conscious – to bring them to full awareness – and to examine the truth of them and discard where necessary or else purify and polish them. We may be motivated by lofty ideals, such as the deepening of wisdom and the unfolding of compassion, but unfortunately we constantly fall short of those ideals. Our human weakness and vulnerability often have the upper hand. We may be unclear and inefficient, irritable or self-centred.

Of all the limbs of the Noble Eightfold Path, Right Vision is perhaps the most difficult to elucidate. It has little to do with intellectual understanding but more with a direct, intuitive, and immediate response to seeing the truth of things. Such penetrating vision may arise as the result of a personal tragedy – when our world is turned upside-down and we are catapulted into seeing things very differently, or it may come from an unexpected experience of tremendous love and compassion that reduces to insignificance all previous similar knowledge. Yet Right Vision does not necessarily have to arise though great turbulence or eruption of emotion. It can arise more gradually, through reflecting on how the world and our experiences are impermanent, insubstantial, and unsatisfactory.

We might, for example, have felt when we first found a particular form of work that the material gains it would bring us, or the status it bestowed on us, or the satisfaction it gave us would provide a sense of meaning that would sustain us throughout our lives. But we notice that gradually, or occasionally, or perhaps even most of the time, we feel there is still something missing – either a little something or a great gaping big something. It might be tempting at this point to think that total satisfaction or meaning lies somewhere clse and go off in search of it, and sometimes we may need to do just that – but not without reflection or we might be missing the point. If we can see that unsatisfactoriness is inherent in these situations, and in all the other 'fixes' that we might try in order to ensure our uninterrupted happiness – such as travel, new skills, education – then we are glimpsing Right Vision.

Right Vision does not stop with seeing the unsatisfactory nature of things; it also brings us another flavour of how things are in their deepest nature: that all things are connected, we are interconnected, intimately bound up one with another. We also see that satisfaction comes not from having (or doing) more and more but by bringing more of ourselves into each thing we do. When we stop planning ahead, or comparing ourselves with others, then we are really engaged with life, with living in this moment – and we are truly alive. Then Right Vision is guiding our actions.

In Chapter 1 I mentioned a checkout girl at a local super-market, and her responsiveness to the customers. It occurs to me that she is intimately connected with a much broader con-text. She is helping to put food on people's tables, she is con-nected to those who've grown the food, packaged and packed it and transported it, as well as to those who buy and eat it. She is part of the huge web of interconnectedness that brings us the food that keeps us alive and is an integral part of life. This may sound fanciful, but how we see our roles and ourselves is cru-cial. If you think about your job as just what you do to pay the rent, or bills, then that is all it will be. If you see it as part of something more, something with a touch of vision, it can be that too.

The world of business is a rich context for the arising of Right Vision, if we are open to it. Every business is operating in a world that is unsatisfactory, impermanent, insubstantial, and wholly outside our control. How easy it would be for Windhorse: evolution, for example, to be swept away by economic or po-litical change. If, for instance, the value of the pound falls against the US dollar, it can have big

This world is extremely unpredictable; everything could completely change overnight.

ramifications for our turnover and profits. If the Indonesian seaports were closed, 35% of our business would be affected, for this is where much of our merchandise is produced. Nothing can be relied upon. This world is extremely unpredictable; everything could completely change overnight. This is a scary thought, but one that Buddhists are positively encouraged to meditate upon. All the efforts we put into making the business a success are firmly held within the grip of the demon of imper-manence. It is by reflecting on this truth and acting in accordance with it that we start to have Right Vision and set out on the spiritual path.

Fay is a young woman whose initial glimmer of Right Vision propelled her to make some radical changes to her life. In 1993, at the impressionable age of 20 and while studying Applied Physiology at Sunderland University, she started attending meditation and Buddhism classes at the Newcastle Buddhist Centre. Within a year a tragedy occurred. Her 26-year-old boyfriend woke up one morning with a terrible headache, and by the evening he had died of a brain haemorrhage. Shocked and distraught, Fay found it hard to maintain perspective. She went to stay with her mother, and while lying in bed nursing her grief, impermanence was all she could think about – all things are impermanent. It was reflections around this truth that lifted her from declining into a deeper depression, got her out of bed, and eventually encouraged her back to her studies. At university, she found that people tended to two extremes: either being in denial of what had happened, or overwhelmed and walking around her as though treading on eggshells. But at the Buddhist Centre she found people who acknowledged the fact of impermanence and death and could empathize with her grief in a very real way, even if they were not entirely comfortable about death themselves. This was a lifeline for Fay.

After she finished her degree, she didn't want to go back to her parents' house and decided to spend more time around the Buddhist Centre. Although interested in her chosen subject, she couldn't see any future for herself in the life sciences and instead wanted to pursue Buddhism more actively. As a consequence, she spent the next nine months unemployed and reading many books on Buddhism as well as browsing literature about other religions.

She was immediately taken with the Dharma, and soon became enthusiastic about it, but she kept asking herself 'Why

Buddhism? Why not other religions?' She felt she couldn't commit herself to Buddhism until she had answered this.

'I remember sitting in the library and drawing up a table in
which I gradually crossed off all the religions that didn't ring
true. I crossed off all the theistic ones, because I didn't believe in
God. Then I looked at the non-theistic ones, skimming the
pages until I got to the fundamental beliefs. The fundamental
principles of Buddhism made so much sense. OK, I thought,
Buddhism is for me, but am I sure about the FWBO?' For the
FWBO had been her only experience of Buddhists practising together, or *sangha* as it is called. She therefore went to test the
waters elsewhere and visited a monastery, where she attended
a day festival which she described as 'all right, but the monastic
lifestyle wasn't for me. Then I read a book by Sangharakshita,
The History of My Going for Refuge, and it was at that point that
everything seemed to fall into place. I remember him saying
Going for Refuge to the Buddha, Dharma, and Sangha – having
these ideals at the centre of one's life – was the definitive act of a
Buddhist, and out of that came one's lifestyle. I could relax.
After that I didn't need anything further to convince myself.'

This time spent considering Buddhism and her faith culmi-
nated, in November 1995, with Fay making a commitment to the
effect that she now considered herself a Buddhist. Shortly afterwards she went on a weekend retreat where she drew up a spi-
der diagram showing how she saw her life at the time and how
she would like it to be. At the hub she placed Buddhism, then in
concentric circles around it she put things like family, friendships, and work. 'I knew there were no other real commitments.
I wanted to live a fully Buddhist life.'

It was seeing an FWBO video newsreel on which there was an
advertisement for Windhorse that persuaded her to change her
life by moving to Cambridge. 'The advert had a "this is where
it's all happening" vibe about it. That's the message that came

across: that's where all the energy is. I've got lots of energy and I needed to engage my energy. Others who knew me well also thought it would be a good place for me to engage myself. So in January I applied for a job, in February I went for a trial period, and I moved there in March. In a way it was all quite impulsive. I'd had some sort of vision and I was following it through. I felt a huge excitement from committing myself.'

What has she since learned about herself? 'I had to develop confidence in coming out with my own thoughts and ideas. Some of these were quite good, which gave me more courage, and others weren't and I had to learn not to take that personally or let it undermine me. I learned I was quite a clear thinker with a good head for figures, and I gradually built up confidence and felt less bothered about being young and inexperienced. Just because people were older than me and had worked for longer, they didn't always know what was best. I think people appreciated my youthful energy. Then came a point when I found myself the most experienced person in an area and was challenged by new people's ideas and their desire to change things to work more effectively. Again I would have to let go of my own ideas if they weren't as good, as well as let go of the assumption that I would always have the best ideas because I had more experience.

'I find that working with numbers has helped clear thinking because with accounting you have to work things through consistently and logically. Developing this faculty is like building a muscle, so when it comes to Dharma study it's been helpful – particularly trying to get to grips with the knottier aspects of it. I enjoy thinking and reflecting, particularly about the nature of existence.... When I first become intellectually clear on some knotty aspect of the Dharma, I feel a lot of joy. The faculty of reason is very important to me. I couldn't commit myself to the

FWBO until I had a good enough reason for it even though I knew in my heart that I would.

'In terms of getting to know myself, being at Windhorse has been like opening up a jack-in-the-box, though it's not always one jack that springs out, but several at once! I've experienced my heavens and my hells. Some of my happiest moments have been at Windhorse and some of my darkest too. I guess the process of coming to work each day is very helpful, because there's certain things that stay the same in the routine of work, so I can compare my mental states with the day before. For example, each morning I switch on my computer and it might remind me of the mental state I was in yesterday when I switched on my computer, and it's different each day. So there are always reference points in the day that stay the same and provide objectivity.

'I could go a lot further with the work I'm doing but it all depends on how much commitment and responsibility I want to take and my feelings around this change. I spoke of being like a jack-in-the-box, all these different parts of me popping out, and I think "gosh, I'm unintegrated!" I can say different things about what I want to do with my lifestyle from one day to the next. Another metaphor I have used recently is it's like being on a carousel, on horseback, going round and round and up and down. My friends are watching me as with one rotation I'm this kind of person, the next I'm that kind of person. And they're waving as I go round just witnessing my unintegration! But even within all this I manage to keep a sense of vision and direction and I know that the conditions here are very helpful for my spiritual growth and development.'

While we only have glimpses of Right Vision, we will of course not have transformed all our actions and attitudes in the light of this. Fay continues, 'I have to say, though, there are some things about being with a group of Buddhist women which I sometimes wonder about. For instance, if we have an office reshuffle, some people have a real attachment to sitting in a particular place and I wonder why people get so emotionally upset about the possibility of it not happening. Someone might say they really want to sit by the window because … and it appears like a good reason, but then I wonder if she's just trying to get her own way. I can use this reasoning as an escape route and wonder if the grass is greener on the other side because I don't have much work experience to compare it to. I don't know what other work situations are like. One of my friends in the office used to work as a social worker and she assured me that people got just as upset when their office was reshuffled. Seems it's just human nature! I guess we're not perfect at Windhorse by any means but we're constantly trying to be more aware of ourselves and others and act in accordance with our vision.'

We talked about idealism, and how it sometimes seems that youthful idealism can become soured or jaded as we age.

'I certainly had a lot of heady idealism when I first met the Dharma. It's still there, but I'm more earthed these days. I still think I can attain insight. I've always thought that. All the reading I did in Newcastle I see as the path of vision. I was really fired up and inspired. Then coming to Windhorse and working it all out in my daily life: that has been the difficult path of transformation, which follows on from the path of vision. I think it's possible to attain insight here, all the conditions are present. There's work, meditation, study, and friendships. All of these involve interacting with other people who provide the love, appreciation, and irritation that are essential for growth!'

Fay was ordained in the autumn of 2002 and given the name Utpalavajri, the blue night-flowering lotus diamond.

5

THE HEART OF THE TRUTH: RIGHT EMOTION

TO MAKE ANY KIND of change in our lives we need three things: to want to make the change, to have the chance to do it, and to know or be shown how to. The key, without which none of it will work, is the wanting to change. We can read self-help books, go on courses, make strategies with our friends, but if our emotions aren't behind the change, we won't be able to sustain it. That is why Right Emotion is stressed at an early stage of the Path; without it we won't be able to follow through on the other steps.

Right Emotion isn't about pretending to be something or someone we're not. The process of transforming our emotions into Right Emotion involves facing up to all of ourselves, discovering what we prefer to ignore and hide, releasing the energy locked up in fear and ignorance. Most importantly, it is cultivating the positive emotions we find within us. The positive can be strengthened when we pay attention to it: when we share our positive emotions and take an interest in finding them in ourselves and in others, they can even grow stronger.

All emotions, including the ones we wish to censure, need to be engaged if we are to make any headway on the path of transformation. We may have dark, murky emotions that we would rather not acknowledge, such as malice or envy, lust or conceit. Denial of conscious emotions needs to be addressed, since keeping hidden and repressed what we inwardly consider unacceptable is likely to do us psychological damage and hold us back in our endeavours. However, our shadow side may be totally unconscious and blissfully obscured for a very long time, even by someone practising Buddhism for many years. It can come as quite a shock to face these unpalatable emotions when the lid is lifted, as it was for Visada after the terrorist attacks on the World Trade Center in September 2001.

American-born Visada has been a practising Buddhist for twenty-four years, first with a Zen group and then with the FWBO in New England. He came to Britain and to Windhorse: evolution in 1994 and since then he has had two distinct jobs, first with the sales team and later with the systems team. He has a love of technology and some self-acknowledged obsessive tendencies, so he poured a lot of time and energy into becoming a self-taught computer expert (as well as a Shakespearean director and actor).

'I rarely used to think in terms of hatred and anger until September 11th. Up to that point, my life had been predominantly pleasant. I was very engaged with work, as though on a seven-year honeymoon. I thought life was wonderful, with the optimistic attitude that if things go wrong they'll get better. Now I see that I was living on a fairly superficial level and that chunks of me were not participating in my spiritual life. As the tragedy unfolded I at first felt grief. But soon I became aware that I was angry, violently angry, and that was a shock. It was quite incompatible with the idea I had of myself. I felt anger towards the perpetrators, but also anger towards suffering, anger towards impermanence, and I lost my love for the world.

'Although I had a strict upbringing, it was a predominantly happy childhood. But there was some strong conditioning of violence that I haven't been addressing in myself. My father, my main male role model, has been a powerful masculine image. He has a third degree black belt in karate, and was in the Army Special Forces Rangers. My Italian-American family has connections with the mafia. A lot of will-power and determination, which I probably learned or inherited from my father, I'd put to the service of the Dharma, while being largely unconscious of my more violent tendencies. I always considered myself slow to anger, but since September 11th anger surfaces in lots of circumstances. I almost got into a punch-up in the street, a thing I'd never have dreamed of before. I've felt "road rage" and "bike rage". The hostility was unleashed by the terrorist events, but it will latch on to other situations, frustrated desire quickly turning to anger.

'When I look back there were clues and a tendency to anger, but I had thought them rather anomalous to my character. At work, I've recently had a number of occasions when I feel the anger rising, particularly when people don't live up to their responsibilities and obligations. For example, one of our shipping companies went into receivership while the boat was on the water, so the container holding our paid-up goods was impounded. I had to try to get it released by dealing with receivers and the shipping company appointed by the receivers. I felt the shipping company was continually giving me the run-around. I realized I should be more direct with them, yet I was feeling angry and raising my voice. I needed to get tough, yet at the same time I was a Buddhist. I couldn't just hammer people, because I knew the anger was coming out of a negative mental state. The company wasn't behaving ethically, yet I had these strong emotions. What was I to do?

'I talked to my friend Rijumati who gave me a few guidelines. He pointed out that there is a difference between getting angry and dealing firmly and without hatred with someone. He advised me not to swear and not to ridicule the other man. He suggested I needed clarity of purpose. If I could harness all the energy I had and stick to the point, I'd be able to catch the other person where they were falling down on their commitment without letting rip my anger and have it slip into hatred. So when I went back to make the phone call, I felt a lot more able to deal with it. I was able to be strong yet clear in insisting he live up to his responsibility. It changed his attitude. He realized he wouldn't be able to carry on buffaloing me, and that he'd have to act in accordance with my wishes. It took a lot of work but was a turning point for me.

'I don't like the feeling of being angry, which is probably why I haven't really owned it in the past, but Rijumati gave me ways in which to deploy that energy so that I could act skilfully. I could put it to the service of accomplishing what I wanted without causing harm either to myself or to the other person. As a result, the anger played itself out, which it might not have done had I gone after the man personally, or repressed it. My predominant emotion was anger, but a "cleaner" anger, which I was able to stop from merging into hatred. Of course, I felt some ill will; after all, the guy was trying to pull one over us, but my speech did not reflect ill will – it reflected strong uncompromising energy.

'The strength of feelings I have since September 11th are far stronger than ever before, and make me think: where has this anger been all my life? I realize there has been quite a lot of me, that hasn't gone along for the ride in the spiritual life, which I'm now coming up against and have to integrate. Though not comfortable, in the long run, I think this is spiritually beneficial. I feel more authentic than ever. If you're not in touch with part of

Padmasuri:
'I see myself as striving, with others, to create a better world.'

Fay:
'I had to develop confidence in coming out with my own thoughts and ideas.'

Vajradarshini:
'If I'm going to do this job I have to engage with it fully, and enjoy it.'

Visada:
'I needed to
get tough, yet
at the same
time I was a
Buddhist.'

Satyagandhi:
'There's nothing
wrong with conflict;
it's how you resolve
it that matters.'

Vajraketu:
'There can be a
certain tension
between running
a successful
business and
promoting the
spiritual welfare
of those involved
in it.'

Buddha mural in the warehouse

Holley: 'It's just as important to bring a person's merits out into the open.'

Katannuta
(with Vijayamala (left)):
'The more I committed myself,
the more freedom I had.'

Sundara:
'Everything ... seemed to make
simple sense which led to a
heartfelt embrace.'

Serena:
'I think about the benefits to the
people in developing countries
who make the goods we sell, how
we affect their communities.'

yourself, it's not the true you, not the whole story. I can't ignore it any more. I'm forced to take this anger and hatred into account in my life, acknowledge it, yet not allow it to have a life in action. In certain circumstances, I need to suppress it, but I'm not pretending it doesn't exist. Feelings of anger have, at times, made me want to cause harm to people – they are very uncomfortable feelings because they are in conflict with my higher ideals. There is a close line between hatred and anger, but I'm learning how it's possible to deploy anger. Perhaps the anger has come about because of the way I've lived my life and I'm reaping the fruits of previous action. I don't need to feed it with new action – that's the trick.

'If I were more developed, I would not necessarily be feeling the anger I do – I'd be firm and direct without the anger. But I'm not at that point of development yet. I'm no longer bubbly and evanescent and happy like I was. My spiritual friends used to say to me, "You're really positive, but I get the intuition there's something more about you." And I'd reply, "You're crazy! When I dig deep down there's just more positivity." That was my experience. Now I'm in touch with all parts of myself, the higher ideals and striving as well as the murkier emotions. One part of me is abhorrent at the thought of wanting to do harm, while the other is actively wanting to injure. I need to integrate the two sides. There's an intense inner conflict between my ideals of love and non-violence on the one hand, and the perception that the "right" thing to do in any particular ethical dilemma (such as what to do with terrorists) might involve violence. I've had to face up to the fact that part of me wants to destroy.

'One aspect of my name, Visada, means "morally dextrous": learning to pick out the right way forward in morally complex situations. With this frustrated anger, I need to sort out what is healthy and what isn't. It may be true that in certain situations violence is unfortunately the best way forward, but that decision must be made out of a desire to do the least harm, not out of feelings of ill will and a desire for revenge. One way or another, I need to harness all my emotions into my life as a Buddhist practitioner. That's the only way forward.'

The emotions we try to keep under lock and key hold a lot of energy that we can release into the work of transformation. Facing up to negative emotions, as Visada pointed out, doesn't necessarily mean letting them spill over, but bringing them into the light of consciousness.

But it is not only negative emotions that can be repressed or hidden; positive emotions can be as well. As Marianne Williamson wrote in *A Return to Love*, 'It is our light, not our darkness, that most frightens us.' We need to encourage and develop positive emotions that we may have neglected, and we need to believe that we can do so: that we are not stuck where we are.

> **The emotions we try to keep under lock and key hold a lot of energy that we can release into the work of transformation.**

Work provides many opportunities to do this. For example, positive emotions such as contentment, gratitude, confidence, and being appreciative and interested can all be engaged in the broader perspective of the task we are doing. Sometimes all it takes is a little time to pause and reflect on our own; at other times it can be very useful to have the input and inspiration that others who are trying to do the same thing can give us.

Other methods of cultivating positive emotions are found in dedicated spiritual practice, such as meditation and devotional practices or rituals. Individuals in the business all have their daily meditation time when they will often be cultivating love and compassion towards others. But we also sometimes engage in collective devotional practices that can really help us contact and develop our emotional feelings towards our ideals. We also learn to hold the vision and the reality of where we are now in equipoise.

Collective practice or ritual makes the transformation of our emotional nature much easier than practice on one's own. I want now to try and evoke the feeling and effect of one such occasion of collective practice: I awoke remembering yesterday's poignant Parinirvana Day ceremony at the Buddhist Centre. This is perhaps my favourite festival of the year, recalling the passing away of the Buddha, and it is also a time to recollect those near and dear to us who have died during the previous year. We shared a few words about the deceased ones with our friends, giving glimpses of their lives.

Now it is Monday morning. I awake to a grey light creeping round the edge of my curtains. It is 6:45am. It is cold, but the heating system is humouring me with its welcome growl. I get up, splash some water on my face, dress, and make some porridge. It is a bit early for this, but I know I will be hungry later if I go on an empty stomach. I eat the porridge, drink some tea, and leave the dishes in the sink. I put on a warm jacket and gloves. The morning fog-filled chill air catches in my throat. I get my bike from the shed and hurriedly cycle down the road. Nobody else is in sight. It is 7:35. I am cutting it a bit close, so once over the footbridge of the swollen River Cam, I pick the pace up through the avenue of trees across Jesus Green, and over Midsummer Common. The fog is certainly thick today: soft greens and blues and greys are merging, fingertips tingle, cheeks feel rosy. I see my breath. I feel good, pleased I had the porridge now. I chain my bike to the railing outside the Buddhist Centre. Phew, I am not the last, but it is 7:45 and we should be starting. One or two friendly faces smile silently in the reception room while we unlace our shoes. I take off coat, gloves, boots, and enter the warm and glowing building.

Yesterday's Parinirvana Day shrine now has some additions: four large golden Buddha figures sit on a plinth draped with gold and red cloths. Twisted willow branches spiral above the Buddhas' heads, plentiful bunches of flowers have been placed at the four corners, many candles are lit, and incense is burning. In a large circle round the base are some seventy individual paper outlines of open hands, each with an eye of wisdom in the palm. Later, each of us will place a candle in each palm. I go down the steps into what had been the pit when the building was a theatre, and as I circumambulate the shrine I see three calligraphic stanzas: 'Cherish the Doctrine, Live United, Radiate Love.' I sit on cushions laid out at the base of the stage. A red blaze of light shines on to the white walls behind me, while right in front of me, resting against the shrine, is a large photograph of an elderly Tibetan monk, Dhardo Rimpoche, the author and exemplifier of the threefold stanza. I look around the circle of men and women already seated, some sixty or seventy of them, some in circular rows set back from the shrine, others on the first tier of the auditorium looking down. I feel a wave of 'coming home', and close my eyes in meditation.

The above stanza encapsulates a theme that Windhorse:evolution has taken up to direct our practice over the next six months. We are marking the start with a ritual: a meditation, followed by a talk by Keturaja on the topic of 'Why themes, and why collective practice?', then concluding with a devotional ceremony consisting of a beautiful sequence of devotional moods. All of us gathered here work in the business. By the end of the ritual, I experience a great sense of communion with the others, so that any chinks of doubt I might be holding about what I am doing with my life just vanish. Here we are, a bunch of very ordinary-looking people wearing all manner of casual clothing, sitting on meditation cushions, with our varying sizes, skin tones, hair colours and styles, accents and dialects, some still very much in their youth, others like me pushing fifty and more. I love it! I feel expanded. I feel thoroughly human.

It is not hard to have an intellectual understanding of the basic principles of Buddhism – not to do evil, to generate love and tolerance towards all humanity, and to understand that all things are impermanent. We can know that grasping after security in terms of material gains is not going to lead to a very satisfying life. All these basic principles are easy to comprehend for anyone who is relatively self-aware and has some understanding of the human predicament. But it is very different indeed to make a real emotional connection between the theory and our practice. Much of the time we are just unable to act in accordance with what we know to be true, because our emotions are not fully engaged in the process of transformation. Consequently, if we are going to make any real progress on the spiritual path, we must bring both our emotions and our volitions into line with our intellectual understanding. It would be difficult to make much progress in Right Speech, Right Action, and Right Effort if our heart is not engaged with that vision.

Right Emotion brings our heart into line with our reasoning faculty, for inspiration to follow the Buddha's teaching will soon run dry, or Buddhism become merely an academic titillation, if our heart is not engaged with it.

6

SPEAKING THE TRUTH: RIGHT SPEECH

WE STARTED with Right Vision, an intuitive response to reality that was then fuelled by Right Emotion. Next we need to encourage that momentary glimpse of a vision to permeate every aspect of our lives. Much of our knowledge is directly or indirectly derived from words, so it seems to me quite logical that a third major component of the path is Right Speech. It is verbal communication that gives expression to both the head and the heart, so in Buddhism a lot of significance is placed on speech.

Lack of real communication can leave us feeling frustrated and one-dimensional. If, for example, people only relate to us at the level of the task we do, or on superficial aspects of our lives, it is likely we won't find our work situation very stimulating or satisfying. It is only too easy for this to happen through busyness, or habitual tendencies, or fear that others won't like us if we show ourselves more fully. I have found that the way to get into deeper conversation is to initiate it. If I am open with others I have found that people will usually respond to me. If I show an interest in others, asking them questions to draw them out, again, people usually respond. It is as though people want more meaningful communication, but they don't know how to go about it. Breaking the pattern involves taking a risk, going into areas where people don't habitually go, but the benefit outweighs these risks – the benefit of a more satisfying life. Such conversation does not have to be lengthy to be rewarding, just heartfelt.

Go into any bookshop and you will find dozens of books covering a wide variety of communication skills, from interaction with work colleagues to how to write creatively. No doubt there are all sorts of useful tips, exercises, and creative ways of using language that can enhance our communication. Standing by our own standards of ethics in speech, and not colluding in backbiting or harmful gossip, repetitive criticisms, or harsh language is as difficult as it has ever been, and just as important. But good communication is not just the fad of the day. The ancient Greek philosopher Socrates placed great importance on reason, logic, and truth, spending time articulating his understanding to a small minority of open-minded Athenian citizens. The thoughts he communicated had a strong impact on the lives of people that continues to this

The way to get into deeper conversation is to initiate it.

day. About a hundred years before Socrates, the Buddha was vocalizing his thoughts and beliefs born out of experience. He was strongly affecting the lives of men and women in northern India, and his influence continues today. The Buddha excelled in communication.

It is interesting to look at how the Buddha was able to have effective dialogue with his disciples. He did not just communicate his own ideas; he also asked appropriate questions and gave praise where it was due. Here is a beautiful example of his simple, direct style. In the *Cūḷagosiṅga Sutta* (*Majjhima Nikāya* 31), we meet three of his disciples who are living together in a bamboo grove. The Buddha comes to visit them and says he hopes they are living together 'in concord, with mutual appreciation, without disputing, blending like milk and water, viewing each other with kindly eyes.' They affirm that they are. The Buddha then asks, 'How do you live thus?' Their answer is quite specific. 'We maintain bodily, verbal, and mental acts of loving-kindness both openly and in private.' He rejoices in their merits saying, 'Good, good!' before going on to say he hopes that they abide diligent, ardent, and resolute. When they again reply in the affirmative the Buddha asks how. Throughout this meeting, the communication remains potent by the Buddha asking pertinent questions not just of the results of his disciples' actions but *how* they are practising. This question of how helps to distil what is effective in the way they are living their lives. Consequently he can be assured by their actions of body, speech, and mind that they are indeed leading a mindful, friendly, and co-operative way of life that is in accord with the Dharma. Then he is fully able to rejoice in their progress.

This is an example of speech that is kindly, helpful, and conducive to clarity and also contains a good deal of Socratic common sense and logic. You can imagine these disciples 'feeling well met' by the Buddha through his very simple, direct, kindly words and questions and a genuine interest in their replies.

In Buddhism, speech is looked at according to four training principles, or precepts, taken on as part of a systematic programme of ethical observance. (Ethics dealing with the body and mind will be dealt with in the next chapter.) Each precept comprises some aspect of speech we strive to abandon, together with a commitment to embrace and cultivate a positive form of speech. These principles, which have universal application, are as follows.

I undertake to abstain from false speech and develop truthful communication,

I undertake to abstain from harsh speech and develop kindly and gracious speech,

I undertake to abstain from useless speech and develop meaningful and helpful speech,

I undertake to abstain from slanderous speech and develop harmonious speech.

I will say a little about each of these and then go on to demonstrate how two friends worked creatively on their communication to address and resolve a conflict.

> Without truthful speech there can be no civilization and culture; indeed there can be no spiritual life and no Spiritual Community.[5]

Truthfulness includes factual accuracy, as well as honesty and sincerity. Truthfulness suggests much more than not telling lies or half-truths. It means saying what we really think and feel – if of course we know what we really think and feel, which we often don't. By clarifying our ideas, we get to know ourselves, and by knowing ourselves, we will be authentic, truthful, and a good friend who can be relied upon. If we don't really know ourselves, if we are unclear and woolly, we can hardly speak the truth, our communication is likely to be inauthentic, and although we might be a warm and friendly person, others will have difficulty in putting their full confidence in us. There may be times when we need to be challenging, even critical, but held within the broader perspective of a desire to reach a mutually deeper understanding of one another – a step nearer the truth. Appropriateness and good timing for such criticism is invaluable as well as keeping the best interests of others at heart. This bears no relation to destructive carping criticism born out of malice.

> The Buddha is passing away, he who is so kind.[6]

When the Buddha died, his closest disciple, Ānanda, chose one quality among the many he might have chosen to describe the Buddha, and that was the quality of kindness. Kindly and affectionate speech involve being really aware of the person to whom we are speaking. To the degree that we are aware and interested in others, we will be able to be genuinely kind towards them. Rather than seeing others as objects and a source of fulfilment for our own needs, we try to see them impartially, not demanding that they be the way we would like them. Kindly speech involves rejoicing in another's merits, that is, speaking openly and wholeheartedly about their good qualities. This creates an infectious atmosphere of positivity. On the other hand, a lot of damage can be done in an instant by some harsh word or phrase.

An example of the difference kind speech can make is given by Holley, who has been working for Windhorse:evolution for about four years. Until recently she was living with her children and husband and commuting a fair distance to work every day. Her husband is in the US Air Force and is away quite frequently on deployments. She came to practise the Dharma partly because it was a way to work with life's difficulties in a more positive way and not get lost in it all. It would have been easier for her not to go out to work; what spurred her on was the chance to make deeper friendships as well as deepen her practice. Within two years, she went from being a purchase ledger clerk to supervising the purchase ledger, as well as other, more difficult, accounting jobs.

'Supervising people wasn't something that came naturally to me – I'm more of a follower. But having been encouraged and supported by more experienced women friends, I've gained confidence in this area. This in turn has had an effect at home, especially in communication with my kids and my relationship with my husband. David isn't a Buddhist, but he has been very supportive. He and I share stories about what we do at work. Of course, this means talking about how we in Windhorse try to work together. He would talk about folks at work and how they would just run one another down – constant criticism but no encouragement. While critical feedback is important, there tends to be an over-emphasis on this aspect in the military. From the day you join, you are reminded in quite a loud and harsh way how you're "not good enough". They call it brutal honesty. It's very easy to put someone down in order to lift your own status, especially if it means you can get promoted. In Windhorse, we make a practice of "rejoicing in each other's merits". This means that while a person may have faults, they have merits too, and it's just as important to bring those into the open. Though we very often rejoice in merits in a ritual context at work, he has taken this idea of "recognizing the good stuff" back to his own team (he is a manager), and from what I understand, people have become easier to work with!'

> Better than a thousand meaningless words collected together, is a single meaningful word on hearing which one becomes tranquil.[7]

It is so easy for our speech to become superficial drivel, which is tedious for others, unhelpful, and often spirals down into negativity. Another unhelpful mode of speech is the cheerless, dispirited kind, especially when it has a dampening effect on others. Any enthusiasm or zest for life just trickles away. It is particularly horrible when I have caught myself having this kind of effect on others – a dismal, pessimistic party-pooper! Meaningful speech, on the other hand, doesn't necessarily imply having intense conversations all the time about the meaning of life. The subject-matter could be almost anything as long as there is awareness of the other person. The first time I met my Buddhist teacher, he spent quite a bit of time – contrary to my expectations – talking to me about the Norfolk weather and skies. He talked about them in such a fashion that I came away feeling far more alive, calm, uplifted, and 'well met' than I probably would have done had we talked about the essence of Enlightenment.

> What he has heard here he does not report there to bring about a quarrel between people.[8]

In stories from the life of the Buddha it is not uncommon to read about disputes between individuals, sometimes the monks, and often over remarkably petty misunderstandings. A graphically descriptive phrase sometimes used is: 'They were deep in disputes, stabbing each other with verbal daggers.' It is the kind of malicious speech that is the result of unskilful, rather selfish, and perhaps jealous states of mind: 'I know better than you.' Speech that promotes harmony is speech that brings people closer together. This means not just being nice to one another, but putting one's own needs and desires a bit out of the way. In the quotation above, the Buddha encourages us not to gossip and defamation which can make an already inharmonious situation more vitriolic. There is a positive counterpart that goes something like this: Alex to Ben: 'Colin has an incredibly good phone manner with customers who owe us money.' Ben to Colin: 'Alex has been singing your praises about what a good phone manner you have with customers who owe us money.'

In other words, someone praises a third party to you. You then go to that third party and repeat the praise. In this way, the person receiving the compliment can be assured it really is praise and not mere flattery – after all, the original praiser had said it to a neutral party. Such a little thoughtful act can bring about a lot of good will and harmony – and it is so simple.

I want to demonstrate how two friends of mine used Right Speech to bring about harmony and concord in a common enough situation of rivalry and misunderstanding. I was very impressed with the way they were able to speak to me about it.

Katannuta works in our accounts team. Satyagandhi now lives in Sydney, but it was not so long ago that she too was working in Windhorse:evolution in Cambridge. It was her first experience of team-based Right Livelihood, although she had been involved with the FWBO in Australia for thirteen years. She and Katannuta worked in the same team in the accounts department. They both have quite assertive personalities and during their shared time in the business they worked through a considerable amount of conflict with each other. I asked them how they came to resolve the conflicts. There was a pause. They looked at each other and broke into a peal of hearty laughter....

Satyagandhi: 'You see, from what we have learned about conflict and resolution we allow the other to speak first!'

Katannuta: 'When Satyagandhi arrived I'd already been working in a large team and my job now was to train her. I had strong ideas about how this "ought" to be, but I didn't find it easy....' Turning to Satyagandhi: '... you being new to Right Livelihood but "old" in the Sangha, new to the purchase ledger but not new to accounting.' Looking back to me: 'I was both training her in the task but also being her buddy in a more general supportive role. We had to work very closely together because it was a complicated job and involved poring over the same bits of paper, using the same computer, discussing how things could be done. I was very exacting and clear in my teaching manner and kept giving the same instructions again and again....'

Satyagandhi: 'And my ego resented the fact that she thought I didn't know what I was doing after she'd told me the first time.' (More peals of laughter.) 'When we talked about what was happening we realized there was this clash of egos. We were both very opinionated, and we mirrored each other in this. What we saw in the other person were aspects of ourselves that probably weren't the most skilful aspects. Once we recognized that we could deal with it.'

Katannuta: 'Despite our opinionatedness we actually got on very well, we were affectionate and cared about each other a lot, yet there was this funny kind of rub. We could have debates about things that were horribly small such as which colour pen you should use to highlight something in a report – it was as basic as that! (But in my own defence I would say that there was a logic in the colour of pen....) They were rather petty things we'd argue about but at the same time we tried hard to develop a friendship. We'd meet up for lunches and spend time together outside work; we even went away together for a weekend. In many ways we were very supportive and friendly towards each other. After a while, we realized that the issues were seemingly about particular things, but in reality it was more about the process of our communication. For instance, there was a way in which I'd say things which would lead Satyagandhi into thinking I was telling her what she "ought" to think, even *what* she was thinking or feeling....'

Satyagandhi: 'At the same time we were able to come together and talk about what had been going on in certain situations and mostly deal with the things as they came up. I don't think we ever went home at the end of the day without dealing with such an issue. We might have to have an hour or two cooling-off period, but also you, Katannuta, were particularly good at knowing when we needed to carry on talking about something and when we needed to stop and come back to it later. I'm not so good at that. I come from a family where everyone argues with everyone else in an excited, challenging way but it doesn't mean anything terrible.'

Katannuta: 'Yes, I'd say "We're having another argument, biff-baff-biff-baff, and it feels horrible!"'

Satyagandhi: 'Whereas I'd say, "No, we're just having a discussion!"' Mutual laughter. 'It was helpful to me to become
more sensitive about when there is more going on for me and
it's not just a friendly discussion any more. There's a pushiness
that comes in, a desire to really push my point home in a way
that's not very caring towards the other person. So I came to
learn to recognize that more.'

Katannuta: 'After a couple of months Satyagandhi knew the
ropes of the job and I had to do a lot of letting go so that she
could just get on with it, for instance decide her own colour cod-
ing rather than follow mine. I didn't find that very easy – I have
been called by my friends a control freak, so it really wasn't
easy.'

Satyagandhi: 'I was competent in the task, which I think made
it easier to let go, but also Katannuta changed jobs so that took
some of the intensity out of the situation.'

I asked them how the rest of the team found the tensions
between the two of them.

Satyagandhi: 'I don't think they had a big problem with it because we would resolve things so quickly rather than let them
build up. It was all in the open. In a way it was so embarrassing
that we just had to do something about it.'

Katannuta: 'I shared the things I felt embarrassed about or
ashamed of and wanted to change. I talked with the others in
our team, or other friends who knew me well, or even straight
to Satyagandhi. I'd want to tell them because it helped my mental states become more "real" for me, particularly the uglier ones
that I'd rather not have to admit to. Sharing my feelings of regret and shame about how I was behaving helped me to remember what I wanted to be like, and to be more committed to
changing my negative states of mind. It also gave people the opportunity to ask me how I was getting on in my attempts to
change, to help me when I was slipping, and to congratulate me

when I was doing well. A lot of the sortings-out between Satyagandhi and me had this confessional element to them. There wasn't a sense of blame: "*You* did this or that." It was much more "This is what I brought to the situation and I'm sorry about it." That's how we were able to contain it in the team without it being a disaster. There was lots of energy, lots of discomfort and dispute, but all that was set within something much bigger. We both aspired to go beyond our limitations and were prepared to work at this. We also laughed at each other and ourselves.'

Satyagandhi: 'Throughout our time working together a lot of trust built up between us because we were able to admit to our own stuff. We could recognize that we were both practising the Dharma. There was also a lot of physical affection between us, we'd give each other little shoulder massages which all helped when trying to sort things out. I discovered quite early on that Katannuta has this great field of energy around her when she's in a bad mood that you feel you can't get through. But I learned that if I were game enough to go through it, put my hands on her shoulders, or give her a hug, it all melted.'

Katannuta: 'Having someone who had the courage to reach right through my defences was huge for me.'

Satyagandhi: 'Forgiveness was easy for both of us because we both wanted to change and give each other the opportunity to do that. We have a similar type of energy. Neither of us felt good when we had these clashes. The way we moved beyond conflict was to take each other more into account in how we did things. We developed a sense of flexibility around each other, letting the other person have more what they wanted. Of course, if we started to do the same job together again we'd probably still argue, but it would be on a different basis.'

Katannuta: 'We learned to be much more aware of how we were putting ourselves across in relation to each other, but it also generalized out into how we related to other people. If someone is saying you're telling them what to do in a way they don't like, it makes you think about your communication with others as well. Especially if the effect I'm having is not at all what I intend to by my choice of speech and language. We had a sharp learning curve in how we put ourselves across and how that affected each other.'

I asked if they would work closely together again if the situation arose.

Both: 'Oh yes!'

Katannuta: 'We have a strong friendship now that would contain a conflict and resolve it.'

Satyagandhi: 'There's nothing wrong with conflict; it's how you resolve it that matters.'

As we have seen, Right Speech has many facets included in the four speech training principles. It is so rewarding to make a real effort in what we say and to maintain awareness of the other person in our everyday conversations, even when we are working out arguments and disharmony.

7

LIVING THE TRUTH: RIGHT ACTION

WITH RIGHT ACTION we come to the heart of our lives – what we do or don't do, what we think, how we respond to our world. Right Action is action that is ethical and bound up with all the small decisions we make in our lives, not just the big ones. Every minute of the day we are faced with ethical choices. Opportunities to be more generous, friendlier, and more encouraging are therefore not hard to find. But what are we talking about when we say ethical?

One of the dictionary definitions of the word ethical is 'in accordance with principles of conduct that are considered correct, especially those of a given profession or group'. Buddhism, however, sees morality as a training principle of intention, and divides ethical observance into conventional morality and natural morality. The external behaviour of someone acting on the basis of these two might look the same, but the mental states behind the action can be quite different. An example of conventional morality would be not fiddling your tax return through fear of getting caught. If you practised natural morality, on the other hand, you would not fiddle your tax return because you regard doing so as 'taking the not given' and you are attempting to move away from the craving mind that wants to appropriate something for its own ends. Someone who is utterly steeped in the discipline of natural morality would not even be tempted to cheat. Natural morality, that which is 'right', conduces not only to a happy, clear conscience (and a good night's sleep) but will ultimately lead to Enlightenment, total freedom. So ethical observance for a Buddhist means disciplining our action, which implies disciplining the mind, the source of all our conscious action.

As with people in the Buddha's day, we are motivated by greed, desiring things and people to bolster our self-esteem, coveting what we think will bring us happiness, and we can spend our lives chasing after things that cannot possibly bring any lasting satisfaction. Another unhappy state of mind is ill will towards others. We might not feel we hate or despise people, and yet how often are our thoughts and conversations critical of others through jealousy, maliciousness, or a general negativity towards the world at large? Furthermore, we are limited by our ignorance. This rather unpleasant triad, bluntly referred to as greed, hatred, and ignorance, is what keeps us repeating actions that only bring unhappiness to ourselves and others. This is what the Buddha perceived. How beautiful and uplifting, therefore, when we hear his words and see his actions demonstrating the opposite of this triad, and revealing his generosity, compassion, and understanding.

Every minute of the day we are faced with ethical choices.

The Buddha makes it quite clear that ethics are inseparable from what we do, and say, and think. Practising ethical observance means reviewing and modifying our bodily action, our speech (which we dealt with in the previous chapter), and our mind and mental states. Ethics in this sense is a vital aspect of work in a Buddhist business. When people speak of ethics in business what they are usually talking about are their social obligations. But Buddhism places the emphasis on personal development rather than corporate responsibility, important though that may be.

There are five training principles comprising Right Action which all Buddhists try to uphold. Each has a negative rendering – of things to abstain from – and a positive counterpart of things to embrace, enabling us to purify our body, speech, and mind. The first is as follows:

> I undertake to abstain from taking life, and with deeds of loving-kindness I purify my body.

This means not only abstention from killing, but from intentionally harming a living being in any way. The non-violent ramifications of this precept are far-reaching and find expression in all the other precepts. Buddhists are encouraged to use their imagination to reflect on the fact that others have the same joys and sorrows as themselves, and to do violence to another in any small way is to negate life. Furthermore, it is not enough to enter sympathetically into the feelings of others; we need also to express our love and friendliness in little deeds of kindness, of which there are innumerable opportunities every day.

Observance of this first precept will naturally result in being a vegetarian. In my mid-twenties I became a vegetarian nearly overnight when I first heard about this precept and pondered its ramifications, although I used to quite enjoy the taste of meat and fish. I had a few cravings in the first couple of months, but I have not knowingly touched meat or fish since then. Many people I work with have taken this precept a step further and become vegan so as to move away completely from the animal industry. Although the ethical perspective of 'not taking life' is the motivating idea behind Buddhists being vegetarian, there is also the whole concern over the processing and transportation of meat.

The arena of personal ethics naturally spills over into attitudes towards the goods we buy and, in our case, the goods we sell in Evolution shops. I will be discussing our buying policies and general business ethics in Chapter 16.

> I undertake to abstain from taking the not-given, and with open-handed generosity I purify my body.

The second precept consists in abstention from not taking the not-given, which is not just abstention from theft, but avoidance of all kinds of dishonesty and exploitation. The positive counterpart is *dāna*, or open-handed generosity. This is the urge to give and share not only material things, but anything, including one's time and energy. Many people who come to work in Windhorse are attracted by the *dāna* element of the business. They are motivated by giving their time and energy to making money for an ideal in which they really believe, rather than into building up personal assets or maintaining a particular lifestyle.

Then there is the less obvious gift of fearlessness. Anxiety is one of today's big problems. We are so attached to things – job, money, car, house, partner, status, financial stability – and our identity is strongly bound up with them. We think these things will bring us lasting happiness, yet there is always the possibility that we will lose them, and in losing them we fear we will lose our identity. Without a larger perspective born of Right Vision, we will always live with this fear. We can give the gift of fearlessness only if we are relatively confident and free from fear and attachment ourselves. By our own understanding that the world is impermanent, insubstantial, and unsatisfactory, and exemplification of our resulting lack of attachment, we help create in others an attitude of fearlessness. It is a most beautiful gift.

> I undertake to abstain from sexual misconduct, and with still-
> ness, simplicity, and contentment I purify my body.

The Buddha said that sexual misconduct comprises rape, ab-
duction, and adultery, all of which are expressions of both craving and violence. For a Buddhist, marriage is considered a
purely civil contract rather than a religious sacrament. Divorce
is acceptable if the relationship is breaking down irrevocably or
is no longer helpful to the spiritual development of those involved. It also means that one is not limited to monogamy if all
partners are in agreement. Polyandry is practised in some parts
of the Buddhist world and is not considered sexual misconduct.
It is also considered fine to be homosexual. On the other hand,
some Buddhists choose to be celibate and are very content with
that lifestyle. The Buddha's philosophy on personal relationships is that they should be based on the principle of non-
exploitation.

> I undertake to abstain from false speech, and with truthful
> communication I purify my speech.

I have dealt with various aspects of this precept in Chapter 6.

> I undertake to abstain from taking intoxicants, and with mind-
> fulness clear and radiant I purify my mind.

Fifthly and lastly comes the precept concerned with purifica-
tion of the mind. If you are unable to think clearly, it is difficult
to speak and act with clarity, and consequently it is hard to practise any of the precepts. Intoxication in any form is therefore
discouraged. While some Buddhists have chosen to be completely teetotal, most others will have just an occasional alco-
holic drink. It is not a rule. If you can drink alcohol and still have
a radiant, lucid mind then all very well, but for most of us alcohol dulls the mind, and part of that dulling is the delusion that
drink has no intoxicating effect on us. The same can be said of
mind-altering drugs. There are other forms of intoxication too,

really anything that obsesses us – the intoxication of youth, or using the remote control to flick back and forth through TV channels, or spending hours mindlessly surfing the Net without much aim or purpose. We all have our pet obsessions, some less innocuous than others.

Mindfulness with regard to the senses is traditionally known as 'guarding the gates of the senses'. All the senses, including the mind, are seen as being like the doors of a house. Just as you might have a guard at the entrance to examine the credentials of anyone who wants to enter, you watch the doors of the senses seeing what impressions, thoughts, and ideas want to enter, and keep out unwanted intruders. If the mind is inebriated with drink, drugs, and tantalizing obsessions, we can hardly keep the lustful, malicious, harmful intruders out.

The ability to act by our own standards of ethics and not be adversely affected by an ethos that does not match our own is not easy. Can we create our own meaning in work to motivate us, even if others don't share it? Can we keep our own standards, working as well as we can at any given task, rather than begrudging the time we spend there and watching the clock, even if that is what others are doing? Can we be friendly and generous to our co-workers, even if that is not the prevailing working environment? These are not easy if we are not supported by others, although this must be the goal we have in mind if our actions are to be Right Action.

I shall end this chapter with Sundara, who was eighteen when he first came across the FWBO in 1993. He was living at home in a village outside Cambridge. He had just finished his schooling, and was smoking a lot of dope and hanging out with his friends.

'I got freaked out doing acid and was uncomfortable around my friends, feeling like I didn't have much street cred. I'd never felt particularly at home in England and I had an urge to get back to my roots, which are in Kenya where I was born and brought up. I had an idyllic childhood going on holidays to the white palm-fringed beaches of east Africa. I'd go on safari and birdwatch and just be out in nature. Something died when I came to England.

'My grandfather had an interest in Buddhism and eastern religion and had bequeathed me some of his books. We'd had a few conversations on Zen philosophy and from that I knew that if ever I was in trouble there'd be truth to be found in Buddhism. I was in trouble so I read those books.'

One of those books was called *At the Feet of the Master*, by a disciple of Krishnamurti. Through this book Sundara became very attracted to the Buddhist approach to ethics, which emphasized that the action was not an end in itself, but it is the motivation behind an action that makes it pure or impure.

'All my earlier desires to lead the simple life, which had been ignited while living in Africa, converged with this ideal of purity.'

His reading motivated him to look for a Buddhist group in the phone book, which led him to the Buddhist centre where he learned to meditate. He signed up for a course on Buddhism and had dinner in a neighbouring men's community the same day. The following week, during the course, he asked if he could work with other Buddhists since he was concerned that if he returned to his friends he would fall back into dope-smoking and that his advances into this new world would disappear. Nothing blocked his way. Within a week of his first contact with Buddhists, he started work in a temporary Christmas Evolution shop.

'Everything I came across in the FWBO was exciting and new, and seemed to make simple sense which led to a heartfelt embrace. On my first retreat, I felt as though I was in a monastery, especially with so many people meditating together in the shrine-room. I was particularly struck by the harmony and relative depth of communication amidst such a large collection of people, and the care they took in relating to one another; there was physical affection and eye-contact for instance. Despite feeling a bit swamped by the whole experience it was pivotal and broadening for me.'

On his return, he threw out the marijuana plants he was growing in his bedroom, stopped smoking, and went to live in a community of nine other Buddhists. He worked in Windhorse for the next seven years, during which time he was ordained and given his name, which means 'beautiful, agreeable, one who shines brightly'.

8

WORKING WITH THE TRUTH:
RIGHT LIVELIHOOD

THERE IS A STORY of three bricklayers who are building a wall. A passer-by asks each in turn what they are doing. The first replies, 'I'm building a wall.' The second replies, 'I'm making money to support my wife and family.' The third replies, 'I'm building a cathedral.' Motivation is the essential distinction here. Similarly, there is a world of difference between simply selling gifts in a shop, selling gifts purely to earn one's living, and selling gifts from the desire to help all beings towards Enlightenment.

In this chapter I want to explore Right Livelihood itself, the fifth limb of the Noble Eightfold Path. For our work to be Right Livelihood, it has to be ethical. I would argue that for our work to really be part of our Buddhist practice we have to incorporate all the other limbs of the path in our execution of it. Sangharakshita has an aphorism, 'Unless your work is your meditation, your meditation is not meditation.' In the same way you could say if your work is not imbued to some degree with Right Vision, Emotion, Speech, Action, Effort, and Awareness, then your work is not Right Livelihood. We all work for different reasons. It would be interesting to ask oneself, 'If I had enough money would I work at all?' For many people, myself included,

I think the answer would be yes, for work – more than any other activity – galvanizes and channels our energies that might otherwise become dissipated.

Apart from money, different people are drawn to diverse types of work for various reasons, and I will broadly divide these into three groups: those who place social values foremost, others who rate interest value as primary, and yet others who see the context for work as the most important. Jobs with social values foremost would include doctors and nurses, teachers, care workers, and similar such vocations. Interest value means the actual subject or product is of uppermost importance. The range of livelihoods that might come under this heading is as vast as people's curiosity. It could be the enjoyment of working on a computer, becoming a salesman of music CDs or a business executive, or pursuing an interest in fashion or architecture or publishing and so on. Thirdly comes the context in which the working environment is of most importance. You might set up a health club with a bunch of friends not because you are particularly interested in health clubs, but because you really enjoy working with those people. Or you might like primarily to work in the open air, so you choose to become a gardener or an instructor of outdoor pursuits.

We are likely to use these three angles to help us decide what work to do. They are rarely discrete or singular. Someone might chose a job doing data entry in a cancer research institute not because he is specially interested in data entry per se, but the social value and context are meaningful to him. Someone else might choose to have a less supportive context for work such as a job in a poverty-ridden inner London secondary school rather than a more advantaged area, because the social and interest values are foremost. It is a happy coincidence when the interest value is also felt to have a social value, for example if you feel the incentive to promote vegetarianism, and you happen to love cooking, so you work in a vegetarian restaurant. If the social and interest values along with an appealing context all come together, then you have probably found a very suitable livelihood: you like people and are fascinated by physiology and the alleviation of pain, so you become a doctor in a stimulating hospital environment.

To look at what Right Livelihood is in this fullest sense of incorporating all the limbs of the Path, we need to look a little beneath the surface. Most people would regard socially motivated forms of livelihood as coming under this umbrella, for if done in the right spirit not only do they not exploit, but they are of huge benefit to mankind. Unfortunately, though, an outwardly helpful job can be performed with dubious motivation. Buddhists regard the inner abundance with which we perform any task as being just as important as the outward nature of the task itself. We have to be very careful not to be just doing 'good works' when in reality self-interest is uppermost in our minds. Unless the inner motivation changes, resentment is likely to set in, and that is not helpful to anyone. Just as a conventionally beneficial activity performed with ambiguous intention might end up being harmful, a socially 'neutral' job, such as a post office worker, performed with vision and commitment, might be an efficacious livelihood in the Buddhist sense. However, I remember some people being quite upset when I gave up nursing to work in the Cherry Orchard restaurant, because from the outside it seemed to be a less 'worthy' thing to be doing.

> Buddhists regard the inner abundance with which we perform any task as being just as important as the outward nature of the task itself.

Buddhists, of course, are as prone to kudos and self-interest at work as anyone else. It should be remembered that until

Enlightened, when the shackles of the distinction between self and other are broken, our motives for doing many things are going to be governed to a large degree by self-interest. The answer, however, is not to sit back and do nothing, but to use awareness to refine and purify our motivation. Working with others who hold the same values as oneself can certainly assist the refining process.

In Windhorse:evolution there are not many people whose interest value is in the product – that is to say, the gifts we sell – or, say, working on a computer. For the great majority the main motivating factors are the context of working with other Buddhists, and the social value of making money so that the Dharma can be made more accessible to the world. It is these aspects that bring people from all over the world to come and work with us.

I now want to introduce Serena, a remarkable 57-year-old woman from Melbourne, who chose to join the business rather than continue with relief work in Macedonia. Serena had been hired as deputy programme manager for a Kosovo programme. She found herself in the position of setting up a programme, with the help of a few staff, to help thousands of refugees. The refugees had fled to Macedonia for seven weeks in 1999 to escape the bombing and were now returning. The local staff had all been hugely affected by the war and were trying to resettle their families, mourn their losses, and build houses in which to live, as well as work for the organization. International staff, on the other hand, could not speak the languages, and faced the discomfort of living in a part of Europe where nothing worked, including communications. They had to cope with a scarcity of food, infrequent supplies of water and electricity, and continue their activities within security confines. Both the local and international staff had to deal with constantly changing personnel within the teams, for the international staff served only very short terms.

Serena, however, was more used to working under pressure than most, and in the midst of all the strain and chaos she managed to maintain a balanced approach and work relatively constructively.

'I'd learned that if war is outside your door you're bound to have conflict within the organization. Either you are working with people who attach themselves to one side of the battle or the other, or with people who have been through the actual war and as a result are stressed, grief-stricken, and exhausted. A lot of people were unable to work constructively. On occasion, I was able to help those who were stressed, but there was so little time, and a lot of urgent needs. It was my meditation practice that got me through that. I'd been meditating for about four years, and I made it a priority to do half an hour's meditation each morning, even if it was just at the level of staying quiet and being calm. It was my lifeline. I'd be working through till eight or nine in the evening, seven days a week. I stuck in there for six months before taking a break, and stayed for a total of ten and a half months.'

Serena had a question in her mind to which she gave a lot of consideration. It was, 'Am I able to work in emergency work such as that in Kosovo as Right Livelihood?' which is to say, incorporating all the steps of the Buddha's Noble Eightfold Path. She reckoned she had already proved to herself that she could not, at least not yet. She felt that to make more progress on the spiritual path at this stage in her life she would need more time to devote to her personal meditation practice, and to her moment-to-moment ability to bring wisdom, love, and generosity to others.

Serena passed through England after leaving Kosovo, and there she met up with three good friends from Australia who were all working in different parts of Windhorse:evolution. She saw how much progress they seemed to be making, and how much clearer they were about Buddhist teachings, and this convinced her that she would like to experiment with coming to work for a while in the business. In particular, she wanted to have more contact with more Buddhists than was possible in Melbourne.

'I haven't come here for the task. Once I'd learned how to do it, I felt I could concentrate more on day-to-day living a Buddhist life, something for which I had neither the time nor the skill before. There's lots to learn, and working in the accounts team gives me the chance because the task isn't intrinsically of interest to me. One of the things I do, for instance, is broaden my perspective. I think about the benefits to the people in developing countries who make the goods we sell, how we affect their communities, and how we make income for those who sell it in England as well as the money we make for the spread of Buddhism in the west.'

From her experience in Kosovo, Serena also wondered what makes teams work effectively. 'Strange to say, I hadn't cottoned on to the team bit here at Windhorse. It wasn't until my team leader explained that we are a team-based Right Livelihood business that it got me thinking, though I'm still not very clear on the team aspect. But what people do know here is how to develop friendships. In a team, perhaps, it's just practising a close form of how you work in the Buddhist community, and that's extremely helpful. There are few other environments where you have such close day-to-day contact with the same people, being with them through all their ups and downs. Windhorse is a microcosm of the Buddhist community at large, I suppose, but there's a very big difference between the teams in project work and teams here. Individuals are given a lot of leeway. If someone is having difficulties, everyone tries to listen to them, tries to hear them. In our Kosovo team, if someone was unable to get on with other team members, or not showing much motivation in their work, the bottom line was the job. Whether you like it or not, you're going to have to get on with them, or leave.

'It's a good situation here in Cambridge as a Buddhist training place. That's the biggest thing that has come out of it for me. When I'm trying to describe it to people, I say it's a bit like being an apprentice, a live-in spiritual apprentice! There are so many committed Buddhists here. I think it's the only place in the world I could get this intensity of practice. When Aussies think of coming over here they just don't understand it can be positively intensive. I need to make the best opportunity of these conditions while I've got the opportunity.

'I want to join the Western Buddhist Order, especially working within the women's wing, for I see women becoming skilled at being conveyors of world peace, and Buddhism has much to offer in that field. I still don't know how "I" should be a peacemaker. War starts with two people having negative thoughts about each other. That's all it takes. Then they start to operate in the power mode and end up killing each other. If it starts with two people, it starts with one. I have to think where my negative thoughts which might increase conflict are, and how I can overcome them.'

Work can usually be relied on to throw up challenges of one kind of another. Work as Right Livelihood turns those challenges into opportunities for practice. Sangharakshita encapsulated that in a punchy aphorism, 'work is the Tantric guru', and we shall now explore what that means.

Milarepa lived in tenth-century Tibet and was the disciple of a Tantric guru (a revered spiritual teacher). He made a real mess of his early life through learning the art of black magic and using it to kill a number of people, including his relations. When he came across Buddhism, he realized the folly of his ways and that he would have to make monumental efforts to counteract his bad actions. He sought out a guru called Marpa, but instead of giving Milarepa the special meditations and initiations he requested, Marpa gave him hard work. He was made to build a tower, single-handedly, from massive boulders, and just as it neared completion, Marpa would get him to dismantle it and start another. So it went on, day after day, month after month. Milarepa often doubted that his guru was a real spiritual teacher, and was near to despair. Finally, Marpa, who was clearly moved by Milarepa's faith, explained that he had treated Milarepa in this way to help him redeem his previous bad actions. Once purified, he was given the initiations he so wanted. Milarepa went on to spend the rest of his life meditating in remote caves in the snows of Tibet, living mainly on nettles so that his skin turned green, and occasionally coming down to villages to teach the people.

In the Buddhism of Tibet, the Enlightened guru such as Marpa confronts his disciple with both his own shortcomings and with the true nature of things. We do not have Tantric gurus in person, but work can have a similar effect to that of Marpa upon Milarepa, though only if we are as receptive as Milarepa – which admittedly is a tall order.

We may perform very good actions but if we appropriate the goodness of our actions to ourselves, we are likely to fall prey to neurotic energy and to suffer. Roy worked for several years on new computer systems for the business. It was a major project that was important for the growth of the business. He spoke openly with me about his confusion and resolve in this area. On the face of it, he was being very generous, giving his skills to an intensely demanding and complex task, and putting in hours of overtime for no extra money. Yet despite such apparent generosity, he found he was unable to concentrate in his daily meditation practice. He continually had headaches and felt unhappy. Although his team-mates greatly appreciated his work, he told me they sometimes found him unbearably disruptive and exasperating to work with.

It gradually became clear to him that something substantial was wrong. He moved away from computer work and into the warehouse where he found himself much more able to practise mindfulness, and his meditation became effective almost overnight. In the warehouse he was working with good friends, which helped him to enjoy his work more. Even so, he still struggled with work as a spiritual practice. He still had difficulties and resentments towards work. The Tantric guru still had more to teach him.

A further breakthrough came during a solitary retreat. He realized he had been relating to his job as a way of supporting his ego: his energy was locked up in his self-image as an exceptionally successful software professional. He thought about leaving Windhorse, but thought he would be letting down some of his very best friends if he did so. He therefore decided to stay, but on a very different basis: helping his friends instead of the more complex motivation of maintaining his ego. Returning from that retreat he experienced a marked change. He was much more present in the 'here and now', his energy became more available for the task in hand, and his communication became clearer, more friendly, and more straightforward. As a consequence, people started to trust him more, so that within weeks he had been given much of the day-to-day responsibility for running his team.

Through work, Roy came face to face with the Tantric guru. He had to reassess who he was and become aware of his shortcomings. Spiritual friendship was one key to help weaken his egoistic grasping; another was making a distinction between formal ethical behaviour and natural morality: the fact that ethics is primarily a matter of intention. This reflection has propelled him into making not just outward modifications to his tasks, but consequential inner shifts of understanding and a freeing up of his energy.

9

SUSTAINING THE TRUTH: RIGHT EFFORT

THE SPIRITUAL LIFE is an active life. It is so easy in the beginning to ride on the initial eagerness, but as the enthusiasm wanes passivity sets in. I imagine this is why the Buddha chose Right Effort as the sixth limb of the path. We have had a glimpse of a vision of the spiritual life, which has propelled us onto the path of transformation. We have engaged our emotions, become much more aware of truthful speech in the broadest sense, tried to live ethically, and ensured that our livelihood is conducive to development and non-harm. What is also needed is unremitting vigilance to prevent inertia and 'going through the motions' in order to maintain progress on the spiritual path.

We can all appreciate the dignity and grace of an action, whether mundane or sublime, that is well done. Even simple, routine tasks can have a beauty to them in the right hands. I recall the purity of concentration of an Indian friend turning out fantastic chapattis in a slum in Pune, while the sun beat down unmercifully on a tin roof. But for most of us, unfortunately, it is all too easy to do routine, apparently boring tasks or actions more in the manner of an adolescent forced to do the dishes.

The Buddha recognized the tendency towards apathy in his own disciples and would speak of the need to keep striving to liberate the heart from the shackles of greed, hatred, and ignorance, and to fill it instead with the skilful states of generosity, love, and wisdom. He suggested a set of exercises known as the four right efforts: to prevent the arising of unskilful mental states, to eradicate arisen unskilful mental states, to cultivate as yet unarisen skilful mental states, and to maintain arisen skilful mental states. From the time we start on the spiritual path, we need to know and be honest about our own mind and mental states and then begin to apply these four primarily psychological efforts. Every time we suppress a negative mental state (one motivated by greed, hatred, or ignorance) or each time we cultivate a positive mental state (motivated by generosity, love, or wisdom) we change ourselves. We can apply these four right efforts to all aspects of our lives.

To demonstrate how the four right efforts have been a liberating as well as a challenging discipline in the workplace, I want to use the exemplary actions of a Dutch friend, Sanghadasa. Sanghadasa became a picker in the warehouse in a team of four, his job being to pull a trolley up and down the aisles, picking items from the walls of boxes on either side, ticking them off on a list, and transporting them to another part of the warehouse to be packed. He was enthusiastic and engaged.

'It was very routine but I loved it. Basically it was very simple work. I saw part of my task as being mindful and efficient, to be accurate and not to make mistakes. Although we were a team of pickers, the actual work was solitary, so it was a bit hard to get a sense of team spirit. The way I engaged in feeling more of a team was to ensure I'd leave the picking location ready for the next person. I'd leave it in a state that helped the next person to pick properly.'

Very early on in their weekly meetings the team started taking on personal precepts: angles on ethical observance that were relevant to each individual. These personal precepts have both a practical relevance and are also aligned to a higher ideal and aspiration. Sanghadasa began a stock-take of his mental states.

'I realized that before I could formulate a specific precept for myself, I needed to know what I wanted to move away from, and what I wanted to move towards. So I started keeping a diary that I'd carry around with me. After the completion of each picking sheet I'd briefly jot down the mental states, perhaps just one word – for example "engaged", "energetic", "angry", or "flat" – and keep it in my pocket. After a few weeks I saw patterns and had more of an overview of my mind. I learned to distinguish between positive and negative mental states, and started to formulate precepts accordingly. During positive states, I recognized a flow of energy and felt engaged and happy, recognizing that I was not just doing a boring old picking job, but making money for other people. I'd been to India, and made friends there, so to aid the cultivation of positivity I began to think that every item I pick is contributing to my friends. This type of recollection would keep me inspired. At other times, I became much more aware of the negative, of anger or narrow-mindedness, and times of non-engagement. In a way my reflections were quite private things, though we'd share our experiences in the meetings, and the progress we were making. When I was reacting negatively, I wondered if there was any progress at all, then I began to think, well, how do I move away from anger? And I realized that even the thought that I'm aware that I am angry and want to do something to change it is to some degree positive, so I experienced a bit of equanimity.'

Clearly Sanghadasa was practising the four right efforts, preventing and eradicating unskilful mental states while cultivating and maintaining skilful ones. He came to understand that just carrying on working would help prevent more unskilful mental states from arising.

'Doing things and doing them well in order to make things easy for others broadens out my perspective. Doing something for someone else even when in a negative mental state is a good discipline and gradually changes the mental state.'

After a few months in the warehouse, he started working part-time in the kitchen and part-time in the warehouse. A daily vegan lunch is prepared for the eighty or so people working here. Sanghadasa had no experience of professional cooking but Amarasiddhi, the chef, was looking for someone to help him.

'Here was a chance to work more closely with another person. I started to experience some different emotions. It was often hectic and a whole new range of mental states and attitudes emerged, although there was still the same application of mindfulness and awareness. In the beginning, I was very resistant to being trained by him. I had a lot of pride, and would be insulted if he told me what to do. Up surged the anger, and the only way I could deal with it was to be like a block of wood, whereas Amarasiddhi just thought I was being rather quiet! At other times we were very chatty and had lots of fun. Pride is not a very pleasant emotion to acknowledge, let alone speak about, especially to the person who seems to be the source of it! However, for a long time we were in different teams for meetings so I spoke of my difficulties with my team, as I guess he did with his. I'm sure that before long we were both

> **Doing things and doing them well in order to make things easy for others broadens out my perspective.**

aware of what was going on. For him it was a new experience to learn how to train someone and engage in positive communication. We never actually talked a lot about it, we just had to get on with it, for there was a deadline to reach every day. The food was important.'

Once he was in the position of training someone else, Sanghadasa could picture himself in Amarasiddhi's shoes, and began to see it as a way of cultivating the skilful mental states of gratitude and understanding. He realized how difficult it could be to train and correct someone without the other person feeling undermined.

'I now saw how good Amarasiddhi had been, and how much he had learned and improved as the weeks went by. Suddenly I could forgive everything I'd blamed him for, and wrote him a card to say as much, because I could really understand now how he'd done so well with me. Of course he made mistakes and wasn't always subtle in his speech, but his intention was to train, to hand on his knowledge, and to befriend me. In retrospect I could so appreciate that.

'We sometimes talk about treading the spiritual path being like cooking the ego. This was a very appropriate metaphor for me in the kitchen. A cooked ego is one that has refined and suppressed the proud and competitive raw ego. Eventually we need to move beyond even the cooked ego to no ego at all! I had to learn to work with another, to play my part and contribute. It was quite stark in a way. If we weren't getting on well together, the lunch would come out OK, but not as well as it could have been, and we'd leave the kitchen depressed. Whereas if we were getting on well, we'd leave the kitchen harmonious and satisfied with the meal.'

Dwelling on interconnectedness helped Sanghadasa maintain positive mental states. 'There's interconnectedness of which I am just a small part, and I came to realize the whole food cycle is like this too. I had not grown the vegetables, I hadn't dug them up or transported them to the shop, nor delivered them here. I hadn't cleaned the water we use to wash them, and I'm not going to eat all the food myself. So there is a chain and range of activities, and we do them with others.'

Sanghadasa became the main chef for two years, during which time he was ordained and given his Sanskrit name which means 'servant of the spiritual community'. He went on to set up a support team for the business. 'It's a very satisfying way to round off my years here. I can give something worthy to the business rather than just receive. The more I take on now, the more I see how much I've received. I didn't recognize it in the beginning. I was too concerned with sorting myself out. I received lots of help from people and I feel lots of gratitude.

'There's lots of opportunity to practise the Dharma at work, to be wholehearted in what I do, to be generous, mindful, and engage in positive communication. Anywhere in the business I can engage with that, it just takes care and effort. Work provides a mirror, because it's very objective. It's not just how I *feel*, but how I engage my mind and interact with others.'

Sanghadasa remained in Windhorse:evolution for a while longer, but eventually returned to Holland. 'One of the lessons I've had to learn is that things won't always be perfect. I have to accept that things won't always go smoothly or as I expect, and that other people have different ideas from me. I can't control everything, especially people, but I can always make an effort!'

Sanghadasa demonstrates how through Right Effort one can eradicate and prevent unskilful mental states such as anger and resentment, pride or righteous indignation, from arising. It is also through Right Effort that we can enjoy and develop positive states of mind such as gratitude and forgiveness.

10

REFLECTING ON THE TRUTH: RIGHT AWARENESS

LAST SUMMER I was on holiday in the mountains of the Sierra Nevada with a Buddhist friend, along with a group of people I hardly knew. Over a rather extended breakfast, the conversation turned to whether we are able to have an effect on how we respond to a given situation. A friendly debate ensued as to how much command we really have over our mental states.

One couple, Chris and Sue, went off to the sea that day. However, their hired car suffered a flat tyre, which meant laboriously changing it in the heat of the day. They returned in the evening. Chris was excited. 'Hey! What you were saying about being able to affect your own mood really worked. I saw the tyre and normally I would have been really pissed off. Then I thought, things don't always turn out the way you had planned. I could get annoyed, or I needn't. I decided not to. I got out the jack and the spare wheel, changed the wheel, got it done quickly, then went off without feeling miffed at all, and we had a great day!' Chris had experienced how awareness can transform our state of mind. As most moods are the fruits of past actions, we can set ourselves up positively for the future, and we can start today, right now.

Much of the work we do in the shop, for example, is repetitive. We order goods, take deliveries, open boxes, price the goods, stock the shelves, serve customers, and so on. The tasks are relatively simple. From the outside it would be easy to think of them in rather boring, not to say negative, terms, and yet these are ideal conditions in which to become aware of ourselves and gradually develop more positive states of mind. A focused mind is a happy mind, and a creative one too. Our states of mind colour what we think, feel, say, and do.

To come to know ourselves, how our mind works and what we can do with it, is rather like a potter working with clay. Like the clay, the self is plastic and can be moulded into something beautiful. If we are unable to change ourselves, or do not even believe that we can, we cannot have any real and positive impact on society. Without changing ourselves we shall not be able to work any differently from the norm, however skilled and talented we may be. It is this aspect of working on the mind that perhaps above anything else makes for creative work.

Leah works in the Evolution shop with me. Before that she had been studying medieval languages at Cambridge University. As a student she volunteered to help out in the shop once a week. Her main memory is of stuffing fillers into cushion covers ready for sale.

'I remember how much I enjoyed that. I recall writing to the shop team describing how my journey home felt after a morning's work. The colours of nature were brighter, I could hear the birds more, and all my senses seemed intensified. It was that experience together with the people I'd been working with that enticed me to come and work full-time in the shop. It was the people more than the work itself that attracted me, but the whole environment affected me. It felt more real than life at college, more real than anything I'd known before.'

Leah's first tasks once she'd joined the team were basic ones – serving customers, sweeping the floor, unpacking boxes, washing the teacups, and dusting. Then as some people left she took on new areas with broader responsibilities.

'It was a relief coming from the academic world into more practical work. I just didn't want to write another essay! Not that I don't use my head now. I might be sweeping the floor but I think about what I'm doing so it's not only a physical act. And sometimes I plan and lead the Right Livelihood meetings which brings out different challenges.'

I asked Leah how she keeps liveliness and engagement in the daily shop tasks.

'It's not dependent on what I do. My mind can find interest in sweeping the floor – it can be just as interesting as reading about the Holy Grail, which is what I used to do a lot of! The key to mindfulness is being fully present in what I'm doing. I used to read heaps of books about medieval languages in order to write an essay – if the effort was fully immersed in what I was doing then I'd enjoy it. Now when I sweep the floor or make a display it's just the same. I can be completely involved in what I'm doing or not. I can, if I choose, put my body and speech, as well as my mental attitude, in one direction, regardless of the complexity of the task. That's when I'm fully engaged and my energy is flowing, that's when it's really enjoyable. As well as the important detail of tasks we need to develop a broader awareness. For instance, there's the whole aesthetic level of creating something that is pleasing both to me and to others in the knowledge that aesthetics are likely to enhance sales. Good sales increase the profit we can give away – all that is part of the energy and interest, all part of the joy and beauty of mindfulness.

'Sweeping the floor is a good illustration for mindfulness of the body and its movements. It's done at the end of the day when there aren't many customers left and you get the whole floor to yourself. It feels like a dance! I can be particularly aware of how I move, how I need to cover the whole floor, work at it from different angles, bring all the dust together, dance round the floor. Another time when I'm particularly aware of my body is when the shop is very busy, and there are a lot of staff in the shop as well as customers. Some coincidence seems to occur. I might be at the counter, a customer needs something, another team member comes up to me with the very thing I need. It's as though physically I put out my hand and what I need comes into it. An awareness of body, of things, and of others comes into play. A mutual awareness. I tend to be more aware when we are busy and need to act with urgency and speed. When I become unaware I break things, or I bump into things, or I don't notice when someone needs help, or someone walks out of the shop without paying. Unmindfulness has knock-on effects on others and on the business as a whole.

'Speaking of potential shoplifters, I do think awareness helps protect us to some degree from shoplifting. We've had many discussions about security systems and intercoms, and some of those are in place, but I've always tended to think of our awareness as our best protection and deterrent. When several staff are on the shop floor on a busy day, just being aware, they are very visible to customers.'

I asked Leah to talk more about awareness of others.

'If I had to name one spiritual practice at work it would be interconnectedness. Thinking about awareness and mindfulness is a way of seeing that we are all connected as human beings, but also the stock and the tasks are all connected to a broader sense of bringing loving-kindness into the world. When I'm working at the till, or wrapping the goods, I'm sometimes giving a kind of blessing to the customer, thinking "may you be well and happy". It's an awareness of wanting to give to others and developing more positive emotion. I might ask them, "Is this a present for someone?" and in this way get into dialogue. I try to imagine where the stock might be going. Awareness of the customers is like being able to identify with them, imagining myself in their shoes … how this shop looks to them, how would I like to be responded to. Trying to look at us from the outside, and be the customer from the inside. The same applies to other team members, wanting to be kind and in harmonious conditions. Being aware is a good way for that to happen.

'When I'm not aware of others and generally distracted I can feel isolated and separate even when I'm working in close proximity to someone. Yet I can be working on my own and feel connected – feeling part of the bigger picture is not dependent on physically being with someone. I enjoy awareness because it connects me to others. This breadth of awareness can be seen in the stock as well as with people. Say I'm unpacking a range of wooden desk items. It's not just the pen box that I happen to unpack first that is interesting, but all that goes with it – the matching letter racks, picture frame, and bookends that will need displaying together – each enhancing the other. If I'm not mindful in both the detail and the breadth I'm not able to be creative. Being mindful we can create beauty, inner and outer.'

> **Wrapping the goods, I'm sometimes giving a kind of blessing to the customer, thinking 'may you be well and happy'.**

Working in such harmony and beauty is clearly possible and definitely desirable, but what about the disagreements and friction that happen in any team? I ask Leah if she could give tips on being mindful while disagreeing with others.

'Frictions happen, of course. Two colleagues might disagree about a job that needs doing. Mindfulness is about being aware beyond our likes and dislikes. If you disagree you need to thrash out what is the best way of doing something. Mindfulness will help in the decision making. Two of you might be setting up a new display of goods. Is your way better or mine? You could instead think, let's pretend to be a customer – it takes it out of our own preferences and prejudices. If the overall aim is to sell the goods, you need to be mindful of who's going to buy it. At the end of the day you might find the option you didn't choose would have been preferable after all. You can't always get it right. Disagreements of this nature, in my experience, don't tend to be huge problems.'

When Leah was new to the shop she was impressed how calm and unruffled people could be in a busy shop and she put that down to the practice of mindfulness.

'I think exemplification is one of the best trainings in mindfulness, the way others work and their mental states affect others. The shop is a chain, from the delivery of stock, to unpacking, putting stock in the stockroom and in the shop, making displays, selling, wrapping, ensuring satisfied customers as far as possible. A good way to train is to think about this chain and ask oneself, "what have I left undone in the cycle? If I arrived now would I be clear about where I needed to start?" So putting oneself in someone else's shoes is a good training in mindfulness, not wanting to cause confusion or irritation. Talking about it helps too. As a team we looked at levels of mindfulness and the whole team concentrated on certain aspects at the same time. This helped me to engage in it more, become more alive. Hearing others talk about things I wouldn't have thought about helped me to get more out of it than if I was just working it out for myself. For instance, one friend found she easily got speedy. She wanted to be more grounded and did so by feeling her feet on the ground and using her breath as an anchor. I hadn't thought about that but I've since found it helpful – we help each other.'

People go into Evolution shops and perceive that something is different, but they can't usually articulate the difference. Perhaps it's the levels of awareness and friendliness at play that makes a difference. It would be nice to think so! Through the way the teams are functioning they have an effect, as I know when I go into any shop as a customer. I pick up on attitudes of the staff and service quite quickly, and that colours my feelings about a shop as much as the goods within it. Many Evolution customers these days know that the shops are run by Buddhists.

'The knowledge that people know we are Buddhists backs my incentive to be more mindful – that's all to the good. I was working on the till with a friend at a very busy time recently. We were short staffed and a long queue had built up. Everything was flowing well at the counter with the credit cards and wrapping, and little exchanges with customers. A woman arrived with her basket of goods, "I've been watching you two work – you're amazing!" She'd been in the queue, watched us working, and yet hadn't got bored or frustrated with the wait. The fact that we'd been aware of what we'd been doing and enjoying it meant this woman had been enjoying herself too. It all has an affect!

'A big part of my internal work is to keep my ideals alive. A Buddhist image that speaks deeply to me is the open hand of fearlessness. Every time I open one of the shop doors I try to bring to mind this image of the extended hand as a way of touching my ideal of gaining Enlightenment. Fearlessness inspires me, it's something I can become, fearlessness has an effect on my surroundings and on others, it helps me to grow. If I can keep in touch with this vision, then every task is not merely a task, but is connected to a vision of something much greater. Stuffing a cushion or dusting a shelf is connected to reality. It is important for me to keep in touch with that arche-typal level. If I lose that then things begin to break down.'

In 2002 the whole business looked at the practice of mindful-ness in the workplace, and over the months we took on various areas of mindfulness. For several weeks we concentrated on being aware of the body and its movements. We were being aware that when we were walking, we were walking; when sit-ting that we were sitting. When talking to a customer, or open-ing a box, or working on the computer we were just realizing that was what we were doing. And we would report back to each other about how we were getting on with the practice each week. It sounds simple, but how often did I find myself walking from one end of the shop to the other with hardly any con-sciousness that I had done so? Some people looked at particular bodily or verbal habits, ones they did not much like, and thought this would be a good opportunity to change. One example was someone who had a habit of playing with his pen top when sitting at a desk, just flicking the clip. He had broken a number of pens in this way, so he took on the practice of not fid-dling in this way.

Many of us tried to be more mindful in our speech. It is so easy to get into the habit of being vague: 'you know … sort of …'. We shared openly with our team friends the habits we wanted to change, then enlisted their help in changing them by pointing them out, sensitively of course. This takes quite a lot of trust, and I was amazed how open and trusting people were with each other, and also the changes made. These practices may sound small, petty, even insignificant, but they are a good start. If we can change the little things, surely it is easier to change the bigger things, and sharing this with others breaks down lots of barriers.

Awareness of speech led to another important area of aware-ness: awareness of others. One of the greatest things I have learned while working in a team is that not only do we have our faults and our foibles, we also have our enormous resources of goodness, depth, and generosity. When someone new joins the team, they might seem quite two-dimensional at first, but as you get to know them better, you gradually share more of yourself with them. They do likewise with you, and so the richness of that individual is allowed to prosper and thrive. If we are receptive then we are mutually enriched, and we can create something much bigger and better by combining our resources and sharing ourselves than we could on our own. These are the sorts of reasons I work with other Buddhists, people who are prepared to take that leap. I can only describe it as a real joy.

In the next phase of practising mindfulness, we focused on feelings and emotions. Then came awareness of thoughts, watching our moment-to-moment thoughts – where they come from, where they go. If someone stopped me in the middle of walking through the warehouse and asked me what I was thinking, would I even know? Awareness of our thoughts gradually helps lessen the droning mental chatter so that the mind can be stilled, calm and clear like a lake on a still summer evening. This deep inner stillness and outer calm evolves into pristine awareness. And it is from this awareness that higher consciousness, the final stage of the Noble Eightfold Path, begins.

11

BEING TRUTH: RIGHT SAMĀDHI

NOW WE COME to the last limb of the path: Right *Samādhi*. It is
difficult to translate this word. Clear one-pointedness of mind is
the primary aspect, where there is a synthesized flow of all
one's energy, and wholehearted engagement in whatever we
are doing. Nevertheless, for that one-pointedness to be Right
Samādhi, the intensity and focus will be balanced with a sense of
ease and calm rather than wilful, forced concentration of the
mind or body. It may be helpful to use a metaphor. Suppose you
are about to cross the road. If you had little concentration it
would be quite easy to step out without noticing a car and be
knocked over. Too forced a focus on the traffic, on the other
hand, might mean that although you looked carefully for cars,
you stepped out and bumped into the woman pushing her baby
buggy from the other side of the road. However, if you are
focused on your destination, as well as conscious of the dangers
from traffic when crossing the road, while at the same time you
are emotionally and bodily composed and have a broad awareness of things and people around you, you will probably cross
the road with ease and reach your destination unflustered.

Relaxed, balanced concentration is likely to be accompanied by an immense feeling of expansion. In other words, it is not merely a matter of technique that we add on to our lives, although it is likely to start off as that; instead, it is something we become. This spacious one-pointed concentration is an essential forerunner to a fully awakened state of being that sees reality as it is. Most Buddhists are likely to regard meditation as the prime tool through which to concentrate the mind and develop higher states of consciousness, from which insight into reality arises. After all, it was through meditation that the Buddha gained Enlightenment under the bodhi tree 2,500 years ago and became a Buddha. However, not many of us today can dedicate as much time to intensive meditation and through one-pointedness gain insight.

Although most Buddhists I know place much importance on concentrating the mind through a daily meditation practice, most of us have also to work. The issue then is how to develop Right *Samādhi*, at the same time trying to hold down some form of livelihood? Kulananda has given a lot of thought to this topic, so I asked him to talk about it.

'Spiritually speaking, I got a lot more from working in Windhorse than I would have got had I, at that time, gone off and meditated on my own. I just wasn't up to that level of practice then, and I wouldn't have been able to sustain very much intensity. I hadn't yet learned how to work effectively on myself. At first, I couldn't even get my energies going. I was all over the place: sometimes a bit stuck, often rather coarse and negative. I had to refine my energies and get them moving in order to function effectively at work. The responsibilities I carried, and the fact that we had pressing debts to clear, demanded in a very objective way that I work on those aspects of myself in order to live up to the task and meet those demands. Meditation wouldn't have exerted the same objective, and inescapable, demand at that time.

'The effectiveness of this was borne out for me by the way it impacted on my meditation practice. Despite being so busy, I set aside time most years to go away for a month's solitary retreat. What I found on those retreats was that each year my meditation had somehow moved forward. I was able to sustain deeper levels of concentration, year on year, and what I came to realize was that this was because I was working on the hindrances to meditation during my working day.'

There are five recognizable hindrances to concentration. They are the desire for pleasurable sense experience, such as food and sex; ill will, when we are irritable or upset by someone, perhaps feeling we have been mistreated by them; restlessness and anxiety, when the mind is perpetually anxious and the body fidgeting; sloth and torpor when we are assailed by heaviness of the body and blankness in the mind; and doubt and indecision when we prevaricate and lose our motivation. These often semi-conscious resistances tend to be highlighted when we sit down to meditate and attempt to focus the mind. But they are hindrances not only to meditation; they hold back energy in general, so we need to recognize and address them appropriately in our day-to-day life. Kulananda continues...

'At Windhorse I had to be as clear as I could be. The work demanded that I stay on the ball. Of course, time and time again, I'd fail. Especially I could get quite angry and unreasonably demanding of people, but the objective nature of the work meant that when that happened it was pretty clear. Sometimes I could see it, and of course others could see it, so I was forced to work on it. The business demands a lot from you: clarity, brightness, energy, loving-kindness, presence – because you're working with others who hold quite high personal and spiritual standards. So you're confronted by that from moment to moment. You are either living up to it, or you're not. The whole situation feeds that back to you immediately, so you have to get on and work on the hindrances all the time.

'And, of course, working with the hindrances moves one towards insight. Team-based Right Livelihood businesses are very good at generating intensity, which is very difficult for most of us to sustain on our own, and in helping people to maintain an altruistic orientation. Intensity and altruism are two bedrock qualities of the spiritual hero, the Bodhisattva, who seeks Enlightenment for the sake of all beings.

'An important aspect is that the business gives away half its profits. You can't be in it for the money. That helps to purify the motivation. Then there are the needs of your team-mates. Their struggles are very real and need to be met. These collective conditions are spiritually very fruitful. But they need to go hand-in-hand with a sustained intensity of practice. And the fact that Windhorse has at times been very ambitious, and gone for growth and profit under very trying circumstances, has been very good at generating intensity. It's not always a bad thing to be a little short-staffed at work, although that can go on for too long with the danger of people becoming stressed. But when you're short-staffed everyone has to give that bit more, it all becomes more intense.

'Work for the Dharma is strong medicine. I don't see it just as an apprenticeship to meditation, as if meditation alone is the real thing and work is somehow only for those who aren't up to meditating. I believe that it's possible to progress significantly along the Bodhisattva path in a situation such as this. In my own experience, I've found that if I set my heart on work that is skilful, it draws me in the direction of self-transcendence. Not all work would necessarily do that. For instance if I were to work purely to make lots of money for myself, or even just money to support my family, it wouldn't have the same transcendent quality. Of course that's not to say that working here you are necessarily free of egoistic motives such as worldly ambition. It's even probable that you want to achieve something rather worldly. Maybe you want to prove yourself, or even just have fun with a bunch of mates. Most of us have a wide range of mixed motives.

'In my own case, I wanted to *be* someone, to prove myself by making my mark. But I was also very motivated by the aspect of making money for others. I was moved by the work Vajraketu and others were doing in India. I visited India and went on a village tour with Vajraketu when he was giving talks to some of the poorest Buddhist former Untouchables. I was really impressed seeing the impact this work was having and I had a heartfelt response to it. And I wanted to help Sangharakshita in his work – I had a strong response to him too. In the end it was this aspect that got me out of bed in the morning. Self-aggrandizement alone wouldn't have done that, I was just too lazy. So the work helped me to go beyond myself to some extent.'

A key goal of the Buddhist spiritual life is the attainment of spiritual irreversibility or insight. Kulananda describes his understanding of this.

'The idea that we have a fixed, unchanging ego-identity which is "us" with its limited needs and desires – a still centre in a turning world from which we look out on things – is fundamentally delusive. That is not the way things are. It doesn't take much to think that there are another 6 billion people on the planet, all with their own perspective on things.

'The food we eat changes us, likewise the air we breathe and the water we drink. We're in a constant state of flux. I can see in myself that I have changed over the years, both physically and in my ideas and behaviour. Nothing is finally stable or static about us, yet we have this delusion that there is something fixed and solid about us.

'Clinging as we do to a fixed view of ourselves, we suffer. For example, if we over-identify with our job we might find it very painful to retire. We all want happiness and some kind of satisfaction, but real satisfaction can only come from letting go of these views. We have to go beyond our fixed ego-identity to a state of self-transcendence, where we recognize how we are constantly changing and we see how it causes pain to try to keep things the same. That is what we mean by insight.

'Sometimes I use reflections about the nature of things to get me through the day. When things go wrong, for instance, as they always do, I sometimes reflect, well, this is how things are. What can I expect? Just get on with it. Things aren't fixed, so everything can always be improved. That's the secret of creativity – the open dimension of things, their essential changing nature, means that there's always scope to change things for the better.

> **The open dimension of things, their essential changing nature, means that there's always scope to change things for the better.**

'I've found that work, especially work for the Dharma, has the capacity to help me see that, because when I work I have to respond to objective needs rather than subjective desires. That helps me – to some extent at least – to loosen the grip of ego-clinging. Windhorse was set up as a response to objective needs. I think it works quite well at helping to draw people beyond themselves. That's what you're trying to do at work, to give rise – to whatever degree you're able – to active self-transcendence, the Bodhisattva's "will to Enlightenment" for the sake of all beings.

'When you look at the people who have stuck for a long time with Windhorse, you see they've become very substantial people. Almost from day one, you see people benefit. I've seen some come into the business in quite odd states of mind, spiritually immature states, and I've seen them gain spiritual substance. I've seen them gain in confidence, in spiritual understanding and competence, as well as in mundane competence. When I speak of spiritual competence I mean the ability to see beyond oneself by taking others into account and responding creatively to them. So I have no doubt as to the spiritual efficacy of team-based Right Livelihood. But I think it takes a certain temperament for people to throw themselves in long term – it's not going to suit everyone.'

Through work there are also opportunities to make other sorts of breakthrough. There is a classic example that Sangharakshita gives. You spend many weeks trying to do a deal. You put a lot of concentrated energy into it. Then one day, at the eleventh hour, you get a phone call saying the deal is off. At that point you can throw the phone across the room, slam the door, jump up and down, reach for a cigarette or whisky, or shout at your subordinates. But instead you could just reflect, 'This is how things are, things are impermanent, insubstantial, and unsatisfactory.' This could be a chance for a breakthrough into knowing reality, a chance to develop insight. Opportunities such as this occur constantly when all your energy is oriented in one direction.

It is easy to think that meditation is the only Buddhist practice for developing wisdom, but as we have already seen the path of a Buddhist is far broader than this. Meditation is not an end in itself, but a very useful tool for the cultivation of positive mental states.

'One way of speaking of the Buddhist path is to talk of it as the path of ethics, meditation, and wisdom. And these are progressive. Good conduct is the basis of meditation. If your conduct is selfish you won't get very far in meditation, and if your concentration is slack you won't develop wisdom. So, as Sangharakshita has said, if you don't have wisdom, or insight, it's because you don't have sufficient concentration. And if you don't have sufficient concentration it's because your ethics aren't sorted. But even if your ethics are a bit rocky you can at least do something – you can give.

'Giving is central to the life of the business. Besides all the profit that's given away, people practise generosity towards their team-mates, as well as a generous attitude to our customers and suppliers. You are attempting to practise the precepts at work and that's going to feed into your meditation practice. Refining our energy, overcoming the hindrances, feeds into concentration that can then flower into wisdom. It all stems from generosity.'

The *Dasuttara Sutta* (*Dīgha Nikāya* 34) describes a ninefold spiral path, each step of which provides the conditions for the succeeding higher step of spiritual awareness. This spiral starts with good conduct, which leads to freedom from remorse, leading on to happiness, delight, and so on up the spiral to wisdom, Enlightenment itself. 'One state' the Buddha said, speaking of this path, 'just causes another to swell.' That suggests a natural process. If we are practising good conduct, in the sense of ethical behaviour, then we will quite naturally be free from remorse; it is inevitable that if we are free from remorse we will feel an innocent delight, and so on up the spiral to wisdom. All this has stemmed from good conduct, the root of everything. As work is likely to be the biggest part of our lives, if we are acting skilfully and ethically in the workplace then it can be seen as the basis of the path to insight and wisdom.

However, life at Windhorse:evolution can be very busy, and people often speak of this busyness having a detrimental affect on their meditation practice. I asked Kulananda if he could give any tips on how to work with this tension.

'I think the effort required to handle busyness creatively builds spiritual muscle, but it takes practice. Our daily meditation practice may be full of thoughts of work, but the effort to try to calm the mind in those circumstances will inevitably bear fruit. You might not become highly concentrated right away, but the work you do in that situation really pays off when you get away into more supportive conditions. You'll find you've developed more capacity to meditate.

'You can give in to distractions and merely concern yourself with the stuff of work, or you can make an effort to calm the mind. In the city and in the world of business your distractions are likely to be grosser than if you were living in a cave in the mountains. You might not have such gross distractions there, but you will still have to make an effort – that's inescapable.

'For most of us, our mental states are primarily selfish. We need to address that to start with. When we've done that to some extent, we'll find it easier to develop calm. It's fine to lead a full life and to achieve one's goals. This means you have to develop discipline. And team-based Right Livelihood situation can demand that of you, if you go about it in the right way. The effort needed to lead a full life will develop your mind and concentration. Learning how to cope with a large input of material is one of the tasks we can take up.

'It's a tremendous training. I watched Sangharakshita when I was his secretary. I might go to him and say, "I think we need to talk urgently about such and such an issue that has come up." And he'd say, "I don't want to talk about that now. Let's talk about it at three o'clock next Thursday.' He's always very clear about his priorities. He has huge demands, yet he goes about them steadily, unflustered, and maintaining the initiative. It's not easy, but it's tremendously worthwhile.'

I hope I've managed to convey a little of this clear, spacious, one-pointedness of mind, the eighth and final limb of the Noble Path. A Buddhist attempts to put all the limbs of the path into practice in their daily life, and in doing so aims for total transformation of their being. For most of us, there is still a long way to go to let these eight limbs guide every aspect of our lives, being, and consciousness. Yet it is only when we allow such guidance that a fully transformed and awakened state of being is born.

12

TRAVELLER ON THE NOBLE PATH

WE HAVE EXPLORED each of the eight limbs of the Noble Eight-fold Path, looking for ways and means to practise them in the course of a working life. But what would the day of a practitioner of the Path look like in its entirety? How do they all come together – the daily successes and failures, challenges and opportunities?

Although I have worked in the business for more than thirteen years, I'd had no experience of the 'van run', but I was interested to see what it was like for the salesmen, and how they make such work a spiritual practice. I was also interested to meet some of our long-term customers and find out what they thought about us. I therefore decided to go out on a van run, and spent a most enjoyable forty-eight hours with Lalitavajra, 'he of playful determination'. He has been in the Western Buddhist Order as long as I have, twenty-three years, although our paths have rarely crossed. I wanted to get to know him in the guise of a travelling salesman, a job he has done for much of the last nine years. In two days we covered much ground, in terms of both mileage and conversation, and I discovered on the way how he puts all eight limbs of the Noble Eightfold Path into practice....

Morning sunlight streams through pink floral curtains and lands on my neatly pressed white cotton duvet cover which is trimmed with pink lace. The walls glow pink, set off by a deep pile carpet of a darker shade. A white clock radio beside my bed reads 6:17. A grey television near the foot of my bed, the only relief from pink and white, sleeps on. There is no stirring yet from the other occupants of the house. I switch on the kettle, and from a wide choice of tea and coffee sachets, make a brew in a pretty white teapot, and subsequently drink out of a feminine bone china cup. Hmm! Yellow flowers on the cup and saucer must be a mistake, the perfect setting has a flaw; I consider the possibility that Lalitavajra may have a confused pink one in his yellow room next door.

I pile up plentiful curtain-matching, carpet-blending cushions on the bed, and spend the next hour sitting on them in not very concentrated meditation. I try to visualize the Bodhisattva who embodies the quintessence of compassion, Green Tārā. She sits on a blue lotus that rises from a lake of tears, her aura, today, emphatically pink. Soon household noises impinge upon my consciousness: gurgling plumbing, humming radiators, footsteps overhead and on the stairs. I try to stay in the moment but find myself thinking instead about the day ahead, with some little excitement, while the smell of bacon wafts up from the kitchen.

It is early April, and here I am in an old priory converted into a bed-and-breakfast in a hamlet in West Sussex. I arrived last night so as to spend two days on part of a van run in this pretty part of south-east England. The vans are a significant part of Windhorse:evolution. Laden with merchandise, they are driven to gift shops all over the UK and Ireland, from where we take wholesale orders from regular customers. At present we own five of these vans, each kitted out with drawers and shelves containing a sample of every item we sell. Before we had our own shops, the vans were the primary source of our sales. In the early days, we carried a quantity of stock and sold direct. Now, with so many more items, we carry only samples and the orders are dispatched from the warehouse in Cambridge.

It is 9 a.m. on Wednesday. We have just left the house, having eaten a slap-up fried breakfast, without the bacon, served at the old oak dining-room table with a 'Dulux' dog at my feet. We drive alongside grassy verges dotted with daffodils, past duck ponds and quaint thatched cottages.

'You must let me know if you're not OK with my driving. I know it can be a sensitive area for people, difficult to criticize, and hard to be criticized.' I am instantly struck by his awareness of me – an awareness I am to see on many occasions towards his customers – and reply, "So far it seems fine, but thanks for the open invitation because I'm a bit of a nervous passenger at times."

Some fifteen minutes later we draw up the other side of the road from a shop called The Bazaar, and Lalitavajra explains, 'I usually park as close as I can, get the back ready, then go into the shop.'

We go round to the back of the van, and undo the doors that let fly glittery streamers of bead curtains, disco balls, and metallic hoops. We pull them to one side, the steps are lowered, and we climb into the magic of Aladdin's Cave. Windchimes and mobiles dangle and clink from walls and ceiling. Drawers and trays all around the edges, held in place by wooden poles, are now 'unlocked'. A heater is switched on, and the hand-held computer and printer are put on stand-by.

'I get the van all ready for the customer before going into their shop so that it doesn't waste their time. On occasion it can be rather annoying. I do all this preparation and then the shop-keeper says, "Oh, it's best if you park just around the corner."'

All ready for selling, we walk into The Bazaar, and are greeted by an enthusiastic young couple, Richard and Rebecca. 'Sorry we're in a bit of a mess this morning, some of the lights have blown. Rebecca is just going to get some more fuse wire. Do have a look around the shop. By the way, where are you parked?'

'In the lay-by over the road.'

'Oh, it's better if you park just around the corner, the traffic wardens don't much like it there....'

Lalitavajra goes off to move the van while I look around the shop. I am particularly interested to see the sort of shops to which we sell. This one is well laid out and displays a wide variety of gifts, candles, cards, and soft furnishings with an emphasis on wicker-ware. I see a number of our products. The shop is neat, comprehensive, and inviting. I discover the owners have been running it for only fourteen months but the previous owner had dealt with Windhorse for a number of years. Rebecca returns, the spotlights are fixed, Lalitavajra has moved the van round the corner, and so we are ready for business. Richard stays in the shop while Rebecca enters the van.

She is both decisive and methodical, pulling out each drawer in turn, and quickly homing in on items she wants to buy. I am a little dismayed, even somewhat embarrassed, at the dust covering much of the stock, and I am later informed that a lot of dust is created when driving along. Not only is there dust, but cracked, chipped, and broken stock too, which when I thought about it was hardly surprising considering the hundreds of items carried clinking and banging together along the network of motorways, city streets, and country lanes. Anyway Rebecca seemed unperturbed, even commenting in friendly jest to me that you have to have a good imagination when looking at some

Leah unloading a shop delivery

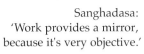

Sanghadasa:
'Work provides a mirror,
because it's very objective.'

Cambridge Evolution
Shop Team

Kulananda:
'The effort
required to
handle
busyness
creatively
builds
spiritual
muscle.'

Lalitavajra:
'I try to see
my whole life
as practice.'

Out on a van run

Rijumati and
Keturaja

Rijumati:
'It's a relief to
be participating
in something
that isn't
to do with
self-seeking.'

'So much of
team work
comes down to
communication.'

Saddharaja and
his son Barney

Ruchiraketu

Soapstone
carvers, Kenya

Allan Hilder

Selling at a trade show

of the goods, just as I found when buying from workshops in India, Kenya, and Bali.

Lalitavajra taps each order into the computer which gives instant information about the quantities in stock. Aladdin's Cave, as I came to refer to the van, is a strange mix of high-tech in a proto-travellers' van, somewhat mirroring the stock we sell, from trendy brushed aluminium picture frames to hand-crocheted dream-catchers. Within half an hour an £800 order is made, instantly printed out, and emailed to Cambridge from the van. We return to the shop and I ask Rebecca how some of the merchandise is selling. We talk about the desirability for better labelling on our products. She is clearly interested in Fair Trade so I speak briefly about our stance. Kenyan soapstone is one of her most popular products. I inform her of the primary school being built in Kisii on the proceeds. 'Oh, that's just the sort of detail I'd like. It would be so good to have more information about such products. People want to know.'

It is time to move on. They seem happy. We seem happy. We start driving and I ply Lalitavajra with questions about the sales team. There are seven men on the vans, divided into two teams. Each person has two runs, and they go out on alternate weeks, making appointments by phone from the warehouse during the intervening weeks. He tells me how there have been recent developments, selling much more to garden and sea-life centres, as well as to zoos, although most of the latter are closed at the moment due to the foot-and-mouth epidemic. Foot-and-mouth is especially affecting businesses in the north of England. Once back in Cambridge, Lalitavajra felt there should be a discussion among concerned parties on how we can help some of the shops in difficulties, such as allowing our regular customers longer to pay. Again I am struck by Lalitavajra exemplifying awareness as well as generosity in his concern for others.

Forty-five minutes later we are driving down a narrow lane flanked by individual suburban houses and bungalows aptly and perhaps predictably called South Lawns, Sunny Dene, The Firs, Chestnut Trees. In front are neatly clipped forsythia hedges and mown verges; gateways and drives are overhung by white and pink cherry blossoms. The van draws up outside Arundel, and as we stop I say, 'How very English this is, you can even hear church bells!'

Lalitavajra laughs, 'There's no church around here, it's the Balinese windchimes!'

We can't hear the chimes while we're driving along, but once we stop, the ethereal sounds from Aladdin's Cave harmonize with surprising melody for several minutes.

We've come to the home of a shopkeeper rather than her shop. This is quite common, though I am still finding it a strange incongruity to see our van in such a middle-class suburban setting. The appointment is for 12:30, and that is the time. However, the house looks very locked up, and so it is. We sit expectantly in the van observing an occasional passing car, but none turn into the driveway. It is 12:45 and we can't wait, so we leave a calling card and continue on our way.

I am enjoying the journey through picture-book villages, and it is a great bonus to spend this time with Lalitavajra. He tells me about his work in Bodh Gaya, the site of the Buddha's Enlightenment in India. He has been supported by the business to spend some of the winter months there during the last three years, running meditation and Buddhism classes for western tourists and pilgrims with a small but growing team. It is to Bodh Gaya that he is slowly turning, a place where he imagines spending many future years.

We eat sandwiches from a service station, and call into a garden centre on spec just because we pass the entrance. I stay in the van while Lalitavajra goes inside, returning within a few minutes, 'A smiley Emma doesn't want to see us, I'm afraid.'

We go back onto the dual carriageway and head east. 'Do you listen to tapes or the radio when you're on your own?' I ask.

'Not a lot except when the cricket is on. I remember one customer who had seen me driving past in the van without stopping, then I returned half an hour later. "Why did you drive past?" she asked indignantly. "Well, there was a very important cricket match on and it was an exciting moment."'

There is no pussy-footing here. Truthful speech is one of Lalitavajra's particular practices. I expect it endears him to many of his customers.

Before long we leave the road and enter the gates of a small seventeenth-century stately home and garden. Driving over a mat of disinfectant and straw, we cruise along a daffodil-lined driveway from which undulating verdant pastures stretch left and right. Grand old trees dot the landscape while casting indigo shadows in the sun-steaming, rain-sparkling grass. We cross a stream and drive alongside an old walled garden.

'Did you see that huge stuffed eagle on the post?' I ask. 'It was surreal.'

'It wasn't stuffed, it was real.'

'Oh, come on!'

Lalitavajra takes the time to listen to messages that have come through via the phone in the van. Paramashanti has phoned through from the warehouse with some price changes, and there is an email listing stock no longer available. Lalitavajra's 70-year-old mother has left a message, as she was to continue to do on a number of occasions the next day, somewhat anxious about her pending move from East Anglia to south-west Wales with which he is helping her.

Lalitavajra sets up the van for sales and we walk over to the house entrance and gift shop. They are not quite ready for us yet, so we are invited to the tea-rooms for a cuppa where we sit watching children paint pictures and young mothers enjoying an afternoon out. Once back inside Aladdin's Cave, a middle-aged woman and a young woman start looking at the stock. Four of us in the van is a bit of a squeeze, not helped by the gradient on which we are poised.

'Oh, it's been a nightmare of a day. Now what have you got that's new?'

'Cats, I imagine you'd sell a lot of cats in a place like this, wooden ones of varying sizes.'

'I don't like cats.'

'They sell very well for most people.'

'No, I don't like them, I'm not going to buy them. What do you think, Tracy?'

'They're OK.'

'Then we'll have six of these ginger ones.'

'What about windchimes?'

'I don't like windchimes. What do you think, Tracy?'

'This one's OK.'

'All right, we'll have four of those.'

They continue in this vein with little apparent method in their buying, often attracted to our lesser-selling items, and I am amazed when their order totals £700. Back down the drive the eagle has flown.

Half an hour later, in oast-house country, we find ourselves outside a semidetached house on a suburban estate. A friendly-looking man comes outside with young boy in tow and says, 'You're bit early; my wife's not back for another twenty minutes.'

'That's OK, we'll just wait.'

'It's better to park the van down the bottom of the road.'

Lalitavajra carefully backs it down. We sit in the cabin for some twenty minutes while Lalitavajra phones his mum. Eventually a smiling round-faced Lisa arrives with a well-behaved little boy in her charge. I ask about her shop in the local market town. I build up a picture in my mind, which is dashed within seconds when she tells me the size of her shop, 'It's about as wide as your van, and three times the length.' That is small!

She asks us what is selling well, and is guided by our recommendations. I enjoy this part, being confident in lines that sell well for us in Evolution, and Lalitavajra gives me the reins. Lisa enquires after Jonathan who usually does this run. He is on a meditation retreat at the moment. 'Oh, I really like him, he's a bit wacky.' Lalitavajra is building up quite an impression of Jonathan, who has been on the vans for a couple of years now. He is clearly proving to have built up good connections with his customers, and is well liked.

Lisa places a substantial order and is happy, though a little surprised at how much she has bought. Lalitavajra gives her the option to lessen some of the quantities, but she declines. When she has gone, Lalitavajra expresses concern that it may have been a rather big order for her, although Lisa had said she was building up her business. I wondered whether I had been a bit pushy, although I had also cautioned her about one or two lines that don't sell very well for us. When selling to small customers, I realize we have quite a big responsibility. Their whole livelihood depends on buying appropriately for their particular shop. It is in all our best interests that they choose well. Lalitavajra told me how he tries to establish whether they are working to budgets. He prefers to have satisfied regular customers rather than big sales.

Once on the road again, I ask Lalitavajra more about how he sees his work as a spiritual practice. He tells me how most importantly he tries to maintain a regular meditation every morning, wherever he finds himself, sometimes incorporating a short devotional practice as well. Then he recites a verse from the *Dhammapada* ('the Way of Truth'), which includes some of the most essential teachings of the Buddha, with stanzas such as the following.

> Look upon the world as a bubble; look upon it as a mirage. The King of Death does not see one who looks upon the world in this way,[9]

'When I first walk into a room in a bed-and-breakfast, I regularly notice all the things I don't like in it. So I start by becoming aware of those things, and aware of my emotional response. It's not until I acknowledge what I'm feeling that I'm able to be creative with it. My mind can get very restless, and it's easy to reach for the TV button. Rather than do that, I've recently taken up the practice of slowly pacing up and down in the room, not blocking out the experience, just experiencing what I'm feeling. Gradually I become more still, more content, and there's less aversion. In simple ways like this I try to practise mindfulness, and it has a positive affect.'

> Experiences are preceded by mind, led by mind, and produced by mind. If one speaks or acts with an impure mind, suffering follows even as the cart-wheel follows the hoof of the ox.[10]

Lalitavajra goes on to tell me how from time to time he practises precepts that help him to be more creative with his time. For instance, the indiscriminate watching of television is a temptation when he is staying in bed-and-breakfasts on his own. Consequently he has sometimes taken a precept not to watch television at all and instead be more creative with his evening relaxation time. While I was with him, Lalitavajra was carrying a volume of poems, *The Rattle Bag*, and reading a couple of poems every evening as well as some Buddhist literature. He finds it important to maintain a connection with beauty, for it is through the contemplation of beauty, which fires his emotions, that Lalitavajra is able to maintain the broader vision and ideal of why he is doing what he is doing.

> Experiences are preceded by mind, led by mind, and produced by mind. If one speaks or acts with a pure mind, happiness follows like a shadow that never departs.[11]

There have been a couple of incoming calls. On a quiet stretch of road Lalitavajra listens to his phone messages. The first one is his mother again. The second is from Vasubandhu calling him from his van run in Ireland. 'I've had an OK day, figures are good, and what's more it's lovely and sunny. Hope it's going well for you, speak to you soon.'

It is getting dark as we arrive in Maidstone, and we find our way with difficulty to the next bed-and-breakfast. Its chatty French-speaking owners make a point of telling us they only like the best organic food and therefore import potatoes and lemons from France (*pommes frites* and lemonade for breakfast?) They try to make us feel at home.

We go out for a meal, and over our buritos and orange juice Lalitavajra talks more about his growing desire to commit himself to spending more time setting up Buddhist activities in Bodh Gaya, combined with a gradual yet inspired move towards a more celibate lifestyle. This conversation leads us to compare notes on times in our lives when 'reality' kicks in, in unexpected ways – times when we saw people in a new light, times when we experienced unfulfilled and deadened longings, which are usually disguised behind the thin veneer of a public mask. We compared this to when the Buddha-to-be, the young Prince Siddhartha, saw in the city streets, as though for the first time, old age, sickness, and death. Yet that was not all that he saw. He also caught a glimpse of a holy man, one who had gone forth in search of truth. It was the potency of these sights that propelled him to go forth himself from home into homelessness in search of truth, and led eventually to his Enlightenment experience.

The following morning we tuck into a continental breakfast of croissant and fruit in a dining room surrounded by a wide variety of original paintings. It is 8.45 a.m. and time to go.

We find ourselves in Maidstone's rush hour, which Lalitavajra negotiates with patience and precision. I compliment him on his driving. We pull into the loading bay round the corner from a shop called Trade Winds and its partner shop over the way. Both are crammed with Windhorse-type gifts as well as colourful clothes, scarves, and jewellery, and the smell of patchouli. They remind me of hippie shops I liked to frequent back in the seventies. Rob, the owner, is a very friendly man who has been dealing with us for years. He is one of those people with whom you feel an instant rapport, rather like one of the family. During the forty-eight hours I was out on the van run, the many customers we met did quite often seem like old friends or family, a network of connections that was much more friendly and intimate than one's usual perception of business associates.

On the road again, I ask Lalitavajra more about his work as spiritual practice. After his morning meditation and devotion, he will mentally 'transfer his merits'. This means he mentally gives away any benefit he might gain from his practice. The aim is to encourage both non-attachment and generosity. He feels this sets him up for the day ahead. He uses Right Awareness to note the various rhythms in the day, watching not just how he is driving and the places he is passing through, but also his various mental states as they come and go.

'I try to see my whole life as practice, and don't distinguish between work and non-work. I just keep going. I'm very aware that everything changes; if I have negative feelings they will change, and I ponder on that a lot. If negative thoughts arise, I can always do something about them rather than just slump. If positive thoughts and feelings are present, I try to maintain them and cultivate them.'

Clearly Lalitavajra is practising Right Effort.

He told me how he tends to reflect on what is called in Buddhism the wheel of cyclic existence. This consists of twelve links in a closed cycle of conditioning factors within which we tend to live our lives, starting with ignorance and ending in old age and death, before the re-emergence of ignorance. Reflection on these links can help us move from just an intellectual understanding to an experience of Right *Samādhi*, so that we can really turn away from craving and aversion.

'I try to dwell in the gap between two of these links, those of feeling and craving, letting myself feel whatever physical or emotional responses are going on, but not letting those feelings tip over into craving or aversion.

'I have developed a number of firm friends in the van team over the years, and each of us in turn has helped each other in many ways. We spend time talking things through with each other. There is a sharing and giving to each other. In our meetings we discuss such things as deepening mindfulness: how we can develop more awareness.

'My work is not just about becoming more professional in the business sense, important though that might be. I need also to keep my broader vision alive and engage my emotions. I need also to become more Buddhist, more committed to the ideals and practice of the Dharma. This encompasses all my activities from driving, to picking orders, to dealing with the accounts, as well as interactions with customers.

'It's a great job out on the vans because I have time on my own when I can think and reflect and ponder on things, then time in the community back in Cambridge which includes time around my friends in the warehouse. We do certain things together so as to be a team, even though much of the time we're on our own. For instance, every Friday evening when I've finished a van run, I meet up with other guys who have also been out, and we go and have a pizza together, tune in with one another, and there are usually a few stories to share. Then during the week in Cambridge we meditate and study together. It's a good life.'

Before long we are in the seaside town of Deal, with Carol, a customer of fourteen years standing. Her small shop, crammed with knick-knacks, is in the front room of her house. We are invited to a cup of coffee in the back room, which looks very similar to the front room. It is easy to see why she must like this business. When a ring on the doorbell informs us that a customer has left, I go back into the shop and chat with her.

'Oh yes, I've known a lot of the Windhorse lads over the years. There was Simon, then John ... oh yes, and then the was the one who drove over the lawn of a neighbour.... Then there was the very good looking one.... Oh yes, then about four years ago there was the one I got angry with. He just stopped calling and there were no phone calls from your office any more. I couldn't understand why, then one day my daughter saw the van passing right by and going to deliver at a neighbour's shop down the road. I was very cross and phoned your head office. There had obviously been some muddle and I did eventually get a very apologetic letter. But apart from that, they are all a very friendly lot. I preferred it when you could buy stock straight off the van, rather than making the order and having it arrive a few days later, but I suppose it's progress and better for you this way. My shop is pretty small but I like it.'

It is lunch time and raining. Carol shuts shop and we all go out into the van while she makes a small order. Lalitavajra and I pick up some snacks from a wholefood store down the road and drive on, Carol waving us goodbye in the rain.

'I used to be very tentative about selling,' says Lalitavajra once back to driving, 'but then Kuladitya came out with me one day and gave me some tips, and away I went.'

As the windscreen wipers swish back and forth, Lalitavajra talks with honesty and integrity. It makes me feel very at ease. He spoke of having a very difficult period soon after ordination, of times when he was unconfident and questioned whether he was really a Buddhist. Slowly he began to see that 'the doubts lay within myself, my own attitudes and insecurities. Buddhism is about transformation. If I wasn't prepared to change, then I shouldn't be involved. I realized I cared deeply and it was time to start *doing* and working on myself. I needed to find something I could give myself to. I had to get on with things and stop sitting on the fence.'

'Windhorse was looking for van salesmen. I agreed to join and it answered all my needs – a new start, a place to live, financial support, and I could do something useful and of great benefit. Later I experienced unexpected benefits – good new friends and a developing sense of purpose and meaning. Over the years I've rebuilt that trust and confidence in Sangharakshita, and in Buddhism, on a firmer footing. I soon began to really enjoy the work. These have been very good conditions for me.'

We are now driving into Ramsgate and the rain is bucketing down. A difficult manoeuvre down narrow streets brings us just around the corner from a florists. I had no idea we sold to florists, but we do. We dash indoors and I am introduced to Heather, a charming woman who has only been running this shop for a short while. Lalitavajra asks her how business is going. 'Oh, it's going well, thanks to you! We need more wooden masks, windchimes, butterflies, wooden cats, and Buddhas.'

She comes round to the van and makes her selection while cradling a larger than life wooden cat off one of the van shelves that she is particularly partial to, while the rain beats down incessantly on the roof.

'I always feel so peaceful being with any of you from Windhorse.'

When the sale is closed, Lalitavajra lends her a leopard-print folding umbrella, a stock item, to get her back to the shop without getting drenched.

'Oh, that's rather nice.'

'You can have it if you like,' says Lalitavajra.

'I'll buy it from you.'

'Just have it.'

'That's so kind of you.'

Off the two of them go to complete paperwork in the shop while I keep dry in the van. A few minutes later, Lalitavajra returns under the umbrella, 'Can you come over and talk a bit with Heather, she's interested in India and wants to know about *But Little Dust*.'

I never did discover how their conversation turned to my book on India, but we chatted about it and about how I had been an ordained Buddhist for more than twenty years. She seemed quite fascinated and hoped she would be able to get a copy of the book. A few weeks later I heard that Jonathan had given her a copy.

'Don't stop coming whatever you do,' she appealed as we bade goodbye.

Our penultimate call of the day was in a neighbouring seaside town. We were heading for the Secret Garden, a fruit and vegetable store in Margate High Street. I was intrigued. The owners had run a florist's in Ramsgate for years and had a long-standing connection with the van salesmen. So now I was to see oranges, potatoes, and cabbages being sold alongside wooden carved male and female Javanese demon protectors. It is very innovative, and I hope it works for them.

It is getting near the end of my trip. I comment to Lalitavajra about the differing perceptions on our stock. For instance, we are carrying some very ornate Chinese vases and planters with a butterfly and caterpillar design. Over the last twenty-four hours different customers have made very different remarks about them. 'They're really funky,' was one, 'Chintzy, they'd go with my curtains,' another, and 'Yucky, it's the sort of thing my gran would have.' It makes me smile. All three possibilities have gone through my mind too, and more. It makes being a buyer interesting.

Anyone can improve any quality by five per cent and the effect, the result, is usually much bigger.

'You build up quite a relationship with your various customers, don't you?' I ask. 'Yes, certainly with some of them. When I'm in India I often send postcards to the ones I'm in good rapport with. Friendliness is something I like to work on, even just being five per cent more friendly is a bit of an aim. It is something tangible to work with, rather than looking at all the many things I need to improve upon. Anyone can improve any quality by five per cent and the effect, the result, is usually much bigger. There are times when we have to make a big effort, big changes, and there are times of steady application and transformation.'

I could see how Lalitavajra's very natural and humble friendliness, which seems to be surrounded by an aura of calm, would be bound to have a noticeable positive impact on people.

We pass through the outskirts of Canterbury with fine views of the cathedral. Lalitavajra will be returning to a bed-and-breakfast in the city this evening in preparation for calls in the town in the morning. Now we are going out to the attractive village of Wye and its well-established and elegant gift shop. I have a good nose around the shop while Lalitavajra talks to Gill. She comes out and looks in the van, has a brief look at some of the new stock, commenting that we seem to have gone very 'youthful' in our look, we need more for older people.

'But really I'm afraid I'm unable to make an order at present. It's like a morgue here in the village and shop at present. There's virtually no custom. About half is due to foot-and-mouth disease, and half this dreadful weather. But I'll come and see your stand at the Top Drawer trade fair in London next month.'

Lalitavajra drops me at Ashford railway station, where we agree on what a valuable time it has been. My probing questions seem to have been useful for Lalitavajra, while the whole experience has been incredibly informative and stimulating for me. I step down from the van for the last time. We wave goodbye as I dash through the rain into the ticket office to return to Cambridge.

In this two-day journey I hope I have been able to convey the practical application of the Dharma translated into the working life of Lalitavajra in the guise of a travelling salesman.

PART THREE

Buddhists in Business

INTRODUCTION

WINDHORSE:EVOLUTION is an experiment in Right Livelihood, one of many in modern Western Buddhism. Different approaches have different flavours that inevitably reflect those who make up the business and those who have shaped it. In this third section we explore some of those aspects that constitute the 'flavour' of the business, as well as issues to do with running a business and its effect on wider society. The themes I have chosen are those we have prioritized or grappled with, and where I have the experience of friends and colleagues to draw on and breathe life into what could otherwsie be abstract topics.

The topics include the importance of friendship at work, teamwork – a key feature of Windhorse – and residential community living, a particular feature for those working in Cambridge. Looking at the wider picture, I ask Vajraketu, the managing director, if principles and profit can coexist. Broadening out even further I look at the question of the impact a business can have on wider society: from the UK to Kenya, India to Bali, and on a wide variety of people from a wood carver to a bank manager.

13

FRIENDS INDEED

> When the heart's release is immature, a lovely intimacy, a
> lovely friendship, a lovely comradeship (*kalyānamitratā*) is the
> first thing that conduces to its maturity.[12]

Friendship is a basic human instinct; children get on with it
quite naturally, on the whole. But it can take a back seat as we
get older and get on with the job of being grown-ups, relegated
to the status of a social extra, not part of the fabric of our lives.
Yet friendship can be so much more. Through giving time, concern, interest, and through sharing ourselves, we become more
human, more connected. It can help us to see that other people,
too, are real; their lives and hopes and fears are as compelling to
them as ours are to us. Real communication is a key route out of
the isolation·and greyness that can creep up on us if we let the
busyness of always 'doing' rule our lives. A friend can make us
feel truly alive in the way that the latest technological gadget
cannot.

Perhaps, as with positive emotions, it can surprise people –
this idea that friendship can be consciously developed, that it's
not something that either happens or doesn't. But friendship
with those with whom we have a natural rapport can go deeper

and we can also develop friendships where we might not have looked for them. In fact, broadening our horizons with regard to friendship can reap many unexpected rewards. The people we work with may well be the people we spend the majority of our time with, and friendship is built on time spent together. Therefore the ingredients for potentially good friendships are already present.

Personal relationships are important on many levels: cultural, psychological, and spiritual. Friendship in the spiritual life has a particular emphasis, the Sanskrit term used being *kalyāṇa mitratā*. *Kalyāṇa* is a word rich in meaning, and connotes such qualities as beautiful, charming, auspicious, helpful, morally good; *mitratā* means friendship. *Kalyāṇa mitratā* is therefore the 'lovely friendship' that can spark genuine communication and exchanges that are mutually beneficial. However, this kind of friendship is not something that happens overnight, and it is not automatic. On the contrary, it can take years and years to develop, and there is no limit to its development. There is a well-known saying of the Buddha in conversation with Ānanda, his close disciple and cousin. Ānanda joyfully proclaims that he has realized that friendship is half the spiritual life, to which the Buddha replies, 'Say not so, Ānanda! Say not so! Spiritual friendship is not half the spiritual life. Spiritual friendship is the whole of the spiritual life.'[13] It is an aspect of spiritual practice on which my teacher has

> **Real communication is a key route out of the isolation and greyness that can creep up on us if we let the busyness of always 'doing' rule our lives.**

placed much importance in his own life and has encouraged in others, suggesting it as one of the keys to human development. It is difficult to make ongoing and substantial progress on one's own. We are trying to create an environment where people can practise fully and wholeheartedly, in friendship and harmony with companions. It is through friendship that we can be encouraged and helped to be wholehearted in our practice.

Vijayamala and I started working in Windhorse at around the same time, she as the accountant while I worked in the shop. At that time there were very few women in the business, and there was a history to our relationship. There was a time when we both lived and worked in India together, and frankly we just did not get on very well. We seemed to rub each other up the wrong way, and probably ended up undermining rather than supporting each other. I felt rather ambivalent about our being thrown together again. However, we had both matured somewhat and we were more secure in our commitment to try to work through the superficial difficulties (which of course can seem momentous when the spotlight is on them). In a way we had no choice. If we were going to work together, we had to address these difficulties. Much water had flowed under the bridge since our time together in India so I think we each viewed the other with a new perspective. We began by just being around each other more, hanging out together, while progressively valuing each other more. Gradually we began to see that we had a common vision of something much greater than just the two of us with our particular peccadilloes.

I well remember driving out to the countryside together for a weekend retreat and getting all fired up about the possibility of setting up a residential community with a number of other women still quite new to the business. A while later it came to fruition. At the time, we both commented how extraordinary it was that a few years previously neither of us would have entertained the idea that we might want to live with the other! Yet we both felt we could now give it a go. It was not always easy. Since it was not an organic friendship, we had to continue to make an effort to develop it. Had we not both been Buddhists, I doubt we would have gone beyond being polite to each other. Yet we maintained a mutual respect and deepened our friendship. Once we were in harmony, we were also able to speak frankly about our past difficulties. Neither of us hung on to our misunderstandings, so we were able to move forward.

We see each other most weeks to discuss issues in the business and how we are progressing with our endeavours. We are also involved in a lot of meetings together, such as the overall management meeting. If we had not had to work together, I doubt that any real progress in our friendship would have been made. But it is not all work. Last weekend, we did a physical work-out class together, sweated in a sauna, then sat in the winter sun outside King's College Chapel eating sandwiches, drinking fruit juice, and watching the world go by and feeling we were on holiday! I greatly admire Vijayamala's commitment to the business – which, now as financial director – is a huge responsibility. I marvel at her love of her many friends and how she maintains connections with people around the world. I rejoice in her good humour and willingness to turn her hand to anything. She is a great exemplar of someone trying to meet the needs of others, and she has initiated new communities for the many Buddhist women who have come to live and work in Cambridge. She is someone with whom I can share whatever is going on with honesty, likewise she with me, and I find her a kind and sympathetic ear in the face of adversity. These qualities are of great spiritual benefit, enabling me to be myself and not hold the lid on things, while helping me to maintain perspective when the going is tough. From difficult beginnings I now consider her one of my closer friends.

Friendships with those people with whom you feel an easy rapport may be congenial, but they are not necessarily *kalyāṇa*. Some such friendships can be based on common needs rather than two individuals becoming mutually aware of each other and relating to the best in the other. Need-based friendships, such as supporting each other's weaknesses in bad habits like heavy drinking, needing flattery in one's style of dress, or shared gripes about a third party, have little to do with *kalyāṇa*.

At the other end of the scale are those people you would hardly conceive of as being your friends and make no effort with at all. I was discussing with another friend how at school we had a tendency to steer clear of certain people almost because we felt that to be associated with them might bring sniggers from others. I cringe when I remember not wanting to be associated with a rather plain-looking girl at school just because she wore National Health pink wire-framed glasses with a plaster over one lens. She wasn't very attractive, and for this reason alone I hardly ever spoke to her. Well, kids will be kids, but this attitude can permeate adult friendships too, albeit in less direct ways. I regard humanity as essentially united despite our different views, culture, language, and so on. Therefore it is surely possible and certainly desirable to be friendly and kind towards any other human being. Without this belief, the world will be governed by hatred, brutality, and war – the hells of earthly existence.

The majority of our *kalyāṇa* friendships are likely to be with others at a similar level of development to ourselves, which we could call 'horizontal' friendships. However, friendship with those more experienced or more developed than us – 'vertical' friendships – can be of great benefit for the spiritual aspirant. My teacher has not emphasized the formal guru-disciple relationship that some Buddhists adhere to, and despite being a teacher and the founder of an order himself, Sangharakshita has considered himself to be primarily a friend to those committed to the Buddhist path. He exemplifies a sense of purpose and direction in his own life as well as forthrightness and concern for the spiritual well-being of others. His determination has rubbed off to varying degrees on all his disciples. Friends who are more spiritually mature kindle the spark of inspiration and confidence, which ignites the vital fire of creativity and potential in our own transformation.

For friendship to be *kalyāṇa* we need mutual awareness, and honesty in how we are feeling and what we are thinking. Friendships need time, courage, and effort. Rijumati and Keturaja, two men who both take a lot of responsibility in the business, demonstrate how the conditions here can greatly aid the growth of *kalyāṇa mitratā*. They have a friendship that has developed over fifteen years, enhanced by living and working together for most of that time. Keturaja talked to me about the development of their friendship, which started in 1988 when Rijumati was studying mathematics and Keturaja was already working in the business.

'There wasn't initially a natural strong mutual attraction, but we got on surprisingly well. We were both at a similar level of involvement with Buddhism and the FWBO. We came from not dissimilar backgrounds, we both asked to enter the Order around the same time, we worked in the warehouse together, and we were just around each other a lot, much more than even most married couples. And we were both idealistic young men with a feeling and a desire for friendship. For me the desire to develop friendship was present in my teens, way before my involvement with Buddhism. When I heard about the ideals of spiritual friendship, it really ignited me and was perhaps my main attraction to the FWBO.

'We were both rather naïve at first. I could be demanding at times, expecting Rijumati to fulfil my unconscious desires, but I was also seeking genuine friendship and intimacy. The two could get mixed up, and the boundaries were not always obvious. It was the same for him, and we'd sometimes fall into strange patterns of relating when one of us was being a bit needy and demanding, and the other would pull back and be wary. We are both strong-willed people with a desire to act out ideals and ideas. It wasn't until we learned to get to know ourselves and each other that the friendship flowed more naturally.

'We have complementary skills, talents, and interests as well as being of different psychological make-up. Sometimes we joke that I'm the more sensitive one, aware of others, while he forges ahead with drive, kind of bull-like, though that's a bit simplistic. Rijumati is very one-pointed, conscientious, thorough, and ethical, always bringing things back to the Dharma. He's very honest with himself and focused in his spiritual practice and doesn't want to compromise. My strengths are a bit different. I think I'm good at having a wider perspective, vision, and direction. I try to be aware of others and how they will respond. I try to draw others in. Of course we haven't always seen eye to eye. For instance, when Right Livelihood meetings were first introduced, Rijumati was very keen on the idea, whereas I had a tendency to anxiety and would say, "There's no time for such meetings; what's the use of them anyway?"'

I commented that from all Keturaja had said, it would seem that those responses were contrary to their individual characteristics.

'Well, that's the thing, it could just as well have been the other way around. It's not really clear-cut. We had a tendency to be quite combative and competitive at times, but from early on there was this sense of having a bedrock of genuine friendship that would see us through times of polarization and difficulties. Even today we can still polarize; we both have a strong will. Sometimes there are areas we're not talking to each other about, but when we realize we attempt to open up. There is nothing I feel I would not be able to talk about with Rijumati, nothing at all, and we often confess breaches of the precepts to each other quite spontaneously.'

They both now have girlfriends, and I asked whether that had made a difference to their friendship.

'For six or seven years neither of us was in a sexual relationship, and then I got involved with Vimalamati, who lived in Sheffield. For me this didn't make much of a difference to my friendship with Rijumati, for we carried on sharing a room, and we saw just as much of each other. It might have affected him more, because I noticed that for a while it lessened my desire to deepen our friendship. Because of our long-standing friendship, I was still open with him and on occasion I found it helpful to talk about my sexual relationship with him in confidence, knowing he'd be supportive. Right through, I felt fairly clear about the different sorts of intimacy I had with each of them, and that I'd be able to retain what I had built up with Rijumati. However, a while later he too got involved in a sexual relationship, and the combination of both of us having other involvements did affect the energy, direction, and desire in deepening our own friendship.

'Yet the way I see it now is that our friendship has gone through phases. In the early stages, we needed each other's support and encouragement, then it became more rooted in enjoying each other's company, and now there's a sense of delighting in Rijumati's many qualities. Not that it's all pleasure and enjoyment; there have been struggle and friction too. In the past, the friendship was a practice. Now we can experience the fruits of all that work in lots of different contexts. Some of the youthful idealism has indeed been realized. That's not to say there aren't still areas where we have to work on friendship, but now it tends to unfold organically rather than the more wilful approach we used to have.

'From very early on, I was convinced that *kalyāṇa* friendship was achievable. Others had talked about it and exemplified it. On occasion my shyness, discomfort, and lack of self-confidence got in the way. This friendship has been more valuable to me than any other relationship I've had, even compared to those whom I look up to spiritually more than Rijumati. Through exploration with Rijumati, I've gained much more clarity about myself than I would just through personal reflection. Our conversations have drawn me out and I think that's been the case with Rijumati too. Some of our best chats would be late at night. This was a time Rijumjati was often more keen to talk than me. I just wanted to sleep! But these were the times we'd casually end up exploring many things: what had happened at work, our interactions with others.... We might speak about people who were having a hard time in the business, or principles of the Dharma, or our meditation practice – all sorts of things.'

For the past year Keturaja wanted to experience himself more separate from the friendship. He wanted to test out more for himself whether he had the ability to self-reflect, and this required having more time on his own. He also wondered whether he and Rijumati had got into habitual ways of relating and wanted to stand back and get more perspective on their friendship.

'In some ways perhaps we are not as close and intimate as we were, but by spending more time apart, I also feel I've gained something. I've become more self-reliant. It's not that I'm pushing anything away, but I've needed to develop something else, away from being concerned with my own needs to more open-handed giving and being more other-regarding, looking out for each other in new ways, so as to be to be an even better friend.'

14

TEAMS AND RESPONSIBILITY

MANY PEOPLE work in teams as a more effective way of accomplishing tasks. I have worked in teams all my life – as a nurse, in a vegetarian café, in India, and in Windhorse:evolution. Teams are fascinating places because you come face to face with other people's ways of doing things and there is much interaction about the best way. We all bring different talents, experience, interests, and personality quirks to the teams in which we work – that both enrich and challenge us – as we grapple with other people's views of reality, life, and work. Teams provide endless, valuable lessons in learning really to get along with people. Living and/or working with someone is quite a test of any relationship. Can we reach harmony with those we work with? Our dreams of world peace don't amount to much if we can't get along with the person at the desk opposite us.

The question of how to function well as a team is one of particular importance when people are trying to work together on some project. Working with others can be a lot more challenging than discussing things with them, say in a study group. In a discussion you can to agree with others at an abstract level (or even agree to disagree) because a concrete outcome is not required there and then. But at work there is a job to be done, so you can't just skirt round the differences in people's approaches.

From a spiritual point of view, therefore, teamwork has much value. Approached in a particular way we can use it to chip away at the protective insecure ego – the 'I' that has to be right, that has fixed ideas about things – and learn to cooperate. In a team we can't always have things our own way, nor can we claim a result as 'ours'; it is the fruit of the work of the whole team, not of one ego. 'I did it' becomes 'we did it'. If our tendency leans in the other direction, to believe that we are invisible, we learn that we do have an effect – as everyone does – for good or ill, and take our responsibility to the team more seriously. It allows us to learn flexibility, to loosen up ingrained habits, and to see others as fully rounded people with their own ideas and desires. We can learn that things look different from different perspectives, and that we all have our strengths and our weaknesses. We can also learn from, and be inspired by, each other.

At Windhorse:evolution our approach is based on teamwork. As we have seen, part of the original vision for the business was to give people a context in which they could work with like-minded people, people following the same path and engaging on a project together. The experiment has grown beyond expectations, but the core of it still consists of teams of people working together. Some of the benefits of this approach to work have already been documented in the interviews. We have seen how it allows us to sharpen our practice by being around others who share our ideals and who may exemplify a quality we have neglected, or by picking us up

> **Our dreams of world peace don't amount to much if we can't get along with the person at the desk opposite us.**

when we fall short of our ideals. Above all, it is very hard to kid yourself that you are further ahead than you are when you are working in a team of people who are mirroring you back to yourself. You may have a wonderful, concentrated, peaceful meditation, but if you then come to work and can't get on with your team members – well, the lessons are obvious.

For a team to work both in terms of the task and as a spiritual practice, its members need to develop and maintain a kindly awareness of each other. Finding ways to remember that each member of the team is an individual with hopes and fears is part of this practice. One of the methods many teams in the business use to maintain awareness of each other is a brief tuning in to each other in the mornings, called reporting-in, with perhaps one time in the week for a fuller sharing of experience. The focus is on anything that might be of relevance for the rest of the team, which might include our own states of mind and being, and how we are progressing or struggling, as well as the objective content of what we have been doing. In the main, these reporting-in sessions are a way to get to know one another a bit more deeply, and to discover and share whatever is preoccupying us.

Naturally, people also meet up with each other individually and might want to explore a particular issue in more depth in an informal context, in or out of work. In the shop, as in other parts of the business, there is a culture of people having lunch breaks in twos, not only with a best mate but with each member of the team. Yet the reportings-in give quite a flavour of the team as a whole, and are beneficial for developing on-going harmony. Every so often we have to re-establish the purpose of the reportings-in, for they can become a little mechanical, or waffly. They might at times also veer towards self-indulgence and inappropriateness. However, the exercise of clarifying their purpose seems in itself to bring a regeneration of enthusiasm to the sessions.

The developments around consciously making teamwork part of spiritual practice came gradually to Windhorse – although looking at the business as it is now, it is easy to assume things have always been like that. But in the early days there was little thought about how to make work a Buddhist practice. Instead, the ethos was more 'just get on with the work'. But many people were not sufficiently motivated simply by making money for Buddhism. Although all the people who worked there were, of course, happy to make money to give away, they needed a broader motivating vision.

People gradually started to articulate a coherent vision of team-based Right Livelihood as a spiritual practice. As Vajraketu says, 'It had been there in the ether, but we hadn't been very strong on understanding and developing it. I'm afraid at the time I thought it a bit feeble! I was willing to go along with it, but for me it was an 'unfortunate' truth. I didn't want reality to be like that. After all, when we moved into the first community there were twelve of us with seven bedrooms in a not very big house. There would sometimes be fifteen of us eating supper and the kitchen-diner wasn't big enough to seat us all, so some had to eat their supper on the stairs, yet nobody minded. We were very gung-ho and idealistic, so against that backdrop it seemed rather mamby-pamby to have special meetings to explore why we were working! I've moved on since then. Now I'm proud that we articulate our two main goals as equal: generating money, as well as promoting the spiritual development of all the individuals in the business.'

Then 'Right Livelihood meetings' evolved. This is where people get together, stepping out of the round of activities and tasks, and look at how we are doing our job. Are we cultivating the qualities we want to emphasize in ourselves? We also reflect on how our work, and our approach to it, plugs in to the broader picture of our lives – our spiritual goal. We can get perspective from stepping back from the bustle of doing, and also by getting input from others on how we are, day to day.

Ruchiraketu was a key player in these developments and spent many years with a particular responsibility for developing the vision of team-based practice.

'In my chats with people the conversation would often naturally turn to how the people in the team related with one another. By attending the weekly team meetings I got a fuller sense of how the team was getting on than I could by talking with people one-to-one. We began trying out procedures and models from the world of business management which we found helpful in clarifying our goals – both business and spiritual. We also used some of these models to explore team dynamics. It was great finding how these models, which had been developed for use in business, could actually be used for spiritual development. For example, in formulating a business plan, it's not enough to have vague aspirations. You need to know exactly what your goals are. The same is true in the spiritual life. If you're clearer about your spiritual goals, you're more likely to meet them. So say you wanted to develop more friendships. You could either just leave it like that, as a vague aspiration, or you could work out the practical steps needed in order to realize it. You could decide that that this would mean, among other things, having lunch with somebody who was new to the business, once a week for a month, starting tomorrow. Such personal precepts would help people make measurable changes to their lives.

'The teams started to set themselves goals, taking a different spiritual theme each week. For example, if the theme was mindfulness, they would examine what effect this had on the number of mistakes in packing orders; in this way the spiritual and the business dimensions of the business coincided. Once the van sales teams started to set themselves targets, for instance to increase sales by fifteen per cent. They did it, apparently without much effort. Until then, sales had been static for years, even though everyone had been sincerely doing their best. This was really exciting. We could be confident that we were definitely making progress because we had measurable goals to aspire to.

'Personally, the thing I found most helpful in exploring ways of working effectively was something called DBM – Developmental Behavioural Modelling. This is a way of looking at ideas and practices with a view to making them more effective, efficient, and elegant. Take the way the same action can mean different things depending on how you think about it. For example, there's a world of difference between thinking that you spend your day in a warehouse in Cambridge, and thinking that you spend it raising money for the Dharma. I found that DBM helped me to understand how the context in which we think makes an enormous difference to our lives. It also helped me to see how you could relate the big picture to specific actions. For example, it showed the relationship between something abstract like mental clarity and the concrete step of keeping your desk tidy.'

In recent years another element in this ongoing development has been introduced with the whole business experimenting with taking up the same theme, rather than each team having a different one. One such theme was the one I outlined in the chapter on Right Emotion, Dhardo Rimpoche's message 'Cherish the Doctrine, Live United, Radiate Love.' Our shop team brainstormed a number of different approaches to that theme over a number of months. These included discussing talks on the subject, reading out extracts from a biography of Dhardo Rimpoche, exploring the notion of a more harmonious team in relation to living united, and having a particular emphasis on customer service while on the theme of radiating love. We thought about introducing silence, apart from essential speech, for one day a week to maintain mindful focus on the theme, and of exploring in one meeting what it means to each of us to be truly human.

These perhaps give a flavour of the variety of approaches available to strengthen our practice of work as a tool for change and transformation. All the teams across the business have both Right Livelihood meetings and time for reporting-in together, as well as a variety of business meetings. I can, however, give only a flavour of these, for they are as diverse, inspired, tedious, elevated, vague, or engaging as the people in those teams make them.

Self-development is a key part of our practice, in teams and in our individual practice. However, there are drawbacks in giving this too much emphasis, primarily that we can get lost in the fog of self-preoccupation. Perhaps the best antidote to an unhealthy wallowing in self-absorption is taking responsibility for things and people beyond ourselves, which, from a Buddhist perspective, includes having faith and confidence in people's innate potential for unlimited growth and development. Responsible individuals take their lives into their own hands, yet they are conscious not only of their own needs and desires but also of the needs, hopes, and aspirations of others. A team valuing every member's contribution does not mean that some team members don't carry more responsibility than others. Working with this – in a context that values everyone's input, and doesn't give greater 'rewards' in terms of salary or perks to those who carry the responsibility – is in itself a practice.

In the shop, as with most teams in the business, we have a team leader with overall responsibility for the spiritual welfare of other team members. Although we do not have an overall manager in the Cambridge shop, we do have a rotating business coordinator who chairs business meetings and is responsible for delegating the tasks for the coming fortnight. We have found this rotation useful in giving people more responsibility and an understanding of the needs of the shop. Some people find delegating hard, while others find being told what to do equally difficult. Switching roles gives a deeper appreciation of what it means both to take and to give responsibility. Within about four months of starting in the business, someone will be expected to take on this responsibility, guided through by a more experienced team member of course. Not all Evolution shops run along these lines. The upside is that it demands a large degree of trust and cooperation. The downside is the possibility of slipping into a false sense of equality and not recognizing that some people are more skilled, wise, or developed than others. Most of the Evolution shops run by teams of men prefer to have a permanent overall manager.

Saddharaja's first experience of teamwork came when it was suggested he could run a Christmas Evolution shop, so as to galvanize people's energies – a shop that is still in business twelve years later. There was no expertise among the few who were initially going to run it, but lots of good will. Saddharaja was able to experience a taste of the sangha at work for the first time and liked it. During that first four-month Christmas period they had a turnover of £42,000, which is amazing when you consider the tiny shop. Profits went, among other things, towards furthering Buddhist activities in Ipswich. On the merits of the financial success, and the enjoyment the team found in working together, they decided to keep a shop on full-time. Saddharaja worked there with friends for more than eight years, while also helping to establish the Ipswich and Colchester Buddhist Centres, living in a community, and being a father to his son.

'I'd lived with people in a Buddhist community before, and met up with members of the sangha one-to-one, but working in a team was a new experience. We were dependent on each other in ways I'd never experienced before: financially, emotionally, spiritually, in terms of friendship, advice, and help in solving difficulties. If any of us wasn't giving to other friends in the team, or if someone became isolated and withdrawn, it was very apparent, so feedback was immediate. I found myself getting closer and more intimate with other team members in ways I'd never experienced before. There was a resonance in our successes and struggles, a positive comparison in our triumphs.'

When at ordination he was given a name that means 'king of faith' he could not relate at first to such qualities, until friends pointed out that his response to life in general and to people in particular was one of faith and confidence, and how such trust had a positive effect on others. He gradually began to recognize those attributes and feel them for himself. For quite a while he was the person most committed to the ideals and practice of Buddhism in the shop, yet business-wise there were others who were better at the job. They therefore took on the managerial and day-to-day running of the business, while he focused more on the people and their emotional and spiritual needs. He had a leadership function looking at the direction of the business as a team-based Right Livelihood venture, rather than solely as a financially successful giftware shop.

'I was interested in and cared about others. That was my strength, and I was able to recruit on the basis of it. Most of the workers were drawn in through the Ipswich and Colchester Buddhist Centres. The main thing that I learned was to be responsible. First I had to become my own man. By taking on a project like this, I was impelled to consider other people and also to get to know myself, which meant going more deeply into spiritual principles and practices, for without that it would be very easy to base one's life on superficial likes and dislikes: doing things the way I like to, with whom I want to work, with my own preferences and prejudices. All that sort of stuff gets challenged when you take responsibility and work in a team. The first thing I encountered when I began to take a lead was unpopularity, which was quite new to me! If we couldn't agree, I had to enter into dialogue so as to clarify spiritual principles and why it might be good to do something in a certain way.'

Taking responsibility gave Saddharaja ample opportunity to reflect on what in Buddhism are called the worldly winds: praise and blame, happiness and sorrow, loss and gain, fame and infamy. Whichever wind is blowing we need not be unduly affected, or knocked off course, but instead try to be unshakeable like a mountain.

'It's very painful if people freeze you out when you are trying to act skilfully, but it does usually come right in the end. In some of my closest friendships, we've gone through this kind of difficulty together and managed to come out the other side. Previously I used to court people's favour; I would pick up the way the wind was blowing and go along with that. But on taking responsibility, I couldn't do that any more – this was new and radical. One person left because they couldn't work with me, though we did eventually make up.'

When some individuals start taking more responsibility, it can happen that others go a bit passive. You see it sometimes with people newer to the spiritual path in relation to Order members. I wondered if Saddharaja had experienced this and how he dealt with it.

'Sometimes it's not a bad thing to let things go wrong and not always be the initiator. I remember a time when the shop team was having a wrangle over the rota. There was a Dharma event that a lot of people wanted to go to, and nobody was prepared to give way. It was a Saturday, the busiest day of the week, and nobody turned up at work except me. I couldn't run the shop on my own, so we didn't open. The following week people felt rather bad about what had happened and such a situation never occurred again. I didn't have to say anything. Everyone saw the consequences of their action. We'd been vague in our communication, almost consciously vague so as to not reach a decision.'

These balances are neither always easy to address, nor even necessarily easy to see very clearly. As well as passivity, there are other burdens that people will lay on those taking more responsibility, either placing you on a pedestal as some kind of demigod, or just as readily pushing you off that pedestal. Either way, they are unhelpfully comparing themselves with you. Saddharaja has had some experience of this in the shop, and even more so when he moved to head office and took responsibility for the spiritual welfare of the men there. The main way he could counteract, though not necessarily prevent, such unhelpful comparisons was to acknowledge and describe his own failures and successes, and remain in friendly communication. He tries not to keep opening up old sores, confesses if he makes mistakes, and along the way develops patience. Quite a tall order!

Saddharaja shoulders a big responsibility in the business. The people who have the most 'spiritual' responsibility and who have a long-term commitment to the business have to be the guardians of the vision of Windhorse:evolution. Saddharaja is one of them. In order to take responsibility, people need to be spiritually mature and understand the overall needs of the business. Someone might come along who would be able to double the sales, but this would be worthless if in the process we lost our spiritual values. The business might become highly efficient, but it would not be Right Livelihood.

Of course, it sometimes works the other way around. You might have someone who is very spiritually committed but can only perform limited tasks. They might be very good at helping and encouraging others to become clear about the Dharma, relating their work to it and behaving by exemplification. People like this might not always take on management roles, but they have an important role in keeping alive the spiritual principles.

Responsibility for others, especially helping others to work creatively in teams, is Saddharaja's great strength. 'So much of teamwork comes down to communication. If it's open, clear, and friendly with a regard for others, then the team will work well and harmoniously, and the business is likely to be successful as a result. On occasion the communication also needs to be challenging. Sometimes people want to reassure you, "Don't worry, it'll be OK," yet that could mean many things. Say we have run out of our best-selling windchimes. That "don't worry" might mean "I've taken care of the situation and it will get better," or "I'm trying not to think about it, forget and hope for the best," or "that's your problem, not mine." It's not clear which it is. It's crucial to clarify through communication. Similarly we can't be vague about Dharmic principles, and the same clear communication needs to take place.'

There are many Buddhists working in Evolution shops who have had previous good jobs and careers, and could go on to what might be considered good career prospects, and some decide to do so after a few years in a team-based Right Livelihood business. Others find working with Buddhists much more satisfying, despite the simple and repetitive tasks.

'Old colleagues from my graphic design days would come into the shop and say, "Hi! What are you doing working in a shop?" with a look of pity on their face. It used to make me smile, because I am so much happier than I was in my career when I had plenty of money and considerable status.'

The responsibility at work might be within the task itself, it might mean taking on other people, and it has to mean taking on oneself. Ideally all three of these areas need to be addressed:

achieving the task we've set ourselves, developing the individual, and at the same time building and maintaining the team. At times one of these may need to be given priority, for instance during the hectic Christmas period, when the task of ordering, unpacking, stocking the shelves, and selling is foremost. If on the other hand one area gets too much emphasis for too long to the neglect of the others, people can become burnt out, or dissatisfied, bored, and possibly resentful. A finely-balanced effort in all three areas is required, and if this happens then individuals are not only going to be stimulated and contented, but they are likely to go beyond the demands of the task, and be genuinely concerned for each other's welfare, as well as taking initiative.

15

SERVICE AND GIVING

'THERE'S A PART of me that wants to let go of that little bundle of selfish concerns – getting "my" pleasures satisfied, getting "my" way – and instead wants to participate in something much bigger. Of course there was a sense of this before I became a Buddhist, before I had really committed myself, but I wasn't mature enough to see it. The vision was too much and it crushed me, whereas these days that sense of awesome sublimity is more tangible and expressed most beautifully in the Bodhisattva ideal. It's the participation in working for all living beings that draws me on.'

These noble words and sentiments are those of Rijumati. He has worked in the business for thirteen years and recently returned from a three-month solitary retreat. He started work here after someone suggested he 'might like to give it a go', so in 1988 he became part of a warehouse team of only three people. 'I counted things and packed boxes and worked on the computer. We were expanding and I became warehouse manager a year or two later. Running the warehouse with what was now a team of seven or eight people was demanding, as several people didn't really want to be there. I didn't have the weight of character to deal with that and would get anxious and frustrated.'

I asked Rijumati whether he experienced any friction between what he was doing, and the way his life might have gone had he followed through his academic career. 'I sometimes thought, well, I've got a degree in mathematics, and here I am packing boxes. It was a bit odd. Although I'd joke about it, I was still wrestling with vocation and career. After all, I'd had one of the best educations that Britain could give, for which I've always been grateful. I thought I ought to be using this, doing something with it....

'Then Keturaja needed someone to work with. I'd been finding it difficult to run the warehouse, primarily because I wasn't up to the kind of communication needed to bring together disparate areas of the team; I'd seriously thought about leaving. I was freed up from my warehouse job in order to help Keturaja. That was a high point, just working with Keturaja. I didn't understand what we had to do, but I was confident he knew what he was doing. I enjoyed just doing what he asked, and not having to react with, 'Hey, I want a say in this decision!' Keturaja has always been two or three steps ahead of me! I was delighted to work for him, driving down to Brighton, unpacking, and setting up with the shop team. It was quite a watershed, marking a breakthrough in terms of individualism. I realized I didn't always have to be in charge, didn't always need to have my say.

'When I was working in the warehouse, my pride meant that I always wanted to have my say, even when I wasn't taking full responsibility for the work and didn't really know what I was talking about! It was this kind of arrogance and narrow individualism that working for Keturaja in 1990 helped to overcome.'

Rijumati then started working as a van salesman.

'In contrast, when I was on the vans I was forced by the nature of the job to take complete responsibility for my actions. If I messed up an appointment with a customer, I couldn't blame anyone else. This made more of a man of me. I knew I was able to make my way in the world and this brought confidence and strengthened my individuality.'

And now? 'Now I feel more and more how beautiful it is when I'm prepared to give up this limited sense of self-seeking happiness for something greater.'

> May the merit gained
> In my acting thus
> Go to the alleviation of the suffering of all beings....
> So may I become
> That which maintains all beings
> Situated throughout space....

These words articulate the desire for Enlightenment for all sentient beings that a Bodhisattva feels, and Rijumati has tried particularly to cultivate the quality of self-surrender they express. 'It comes back to that quality of sacrifice and self-surrender which is just so much bigger than my selfish concerns. If you think about it, it's ridiculous to spend your life building up your personal interests. They're all scattered at your death, so what can make any sense of it? It's got to be something that transcends one individual. So I can see that thread of self-surrender all the way through my life: being attracted to the sangha, going through an existential crisis, and wanting to give myself to something much bigger. The whole practice of serving the Dharma is an expression of it.'

But this does not mean giving up responsibility for oneself. 'There should be no abrogation of personal, moral responsibility to a higher will. The individual must always take responsibility for their actions. Even a direct message from the Buddha must be evaluated to see if it is accordance with the basic essence of the Dharma – how much more so a communication from a human teacher, no matter how respected they may be.

'Through the medium of my work in Windhorse, I feel I am working for and promoting something that is of great benefit: the establishment of the Dharma in Westernized countries. The Dharma has a unique message to offer people who are struggling to find meaning and value in their lives. When I came across Sangharakshita's teaching, it made so much sense to me, and was so clear compared to what I found in the admittedly limited explorations of other traditions. Therefore I want to help this become available to more people. We are about making money to support people to practise and to communicate Buddhism in the West in a form that I feel is much needed in our hyper-consumer and materialist cultures. I think that we badly need a re-evaluation.

'It's a relief to be participating in something that isn't to do with self-seeking. In the *Bhara Sutta* (*Saṃyutta Nikāya* XXII.22) the Buddha refers to the burden of the five *skandhas* – that is, the basic factors that make up an ordinary person. With all our desires and aversions we are constantly buffeted about: "I want this, I can't stand that." The nub of this is the selfish orientation of our perceptions, the self-seeking drives. It is as though one is carrying a huge burden, that of seeing everything in one's experience in terms of whether it is good for you or bad for you. And of course we are never going to succeed in just keeping in the good and pushing away the bad. In the long run, at the very least, death will take us. So to let go of this struggle is like putting down a burden, and when one begins to serve something higher and greater than oneself, this is what happens. Questions such as "why has he got more than me?" or "why aren't they giving me more?" cease to make sense. It's a huge relief!

'Tsongkhapa, the great fourteenth-century reformer of Tibetan Buddhism, calls it the iron net of self-grasping. You're just caught in this net of things of "me": furthering "my" career, "my" skills, and so on. These are real questions that people have to face when working in team-based Right Livelihood on pocket money, neither getting rich nor gaining worldly qualifications. It's a real relief to put that down and find something you truly believe in, that you believe is furthering the teachings of the Dharma. It makes sense of all those pressing questions.'

Most people face doubts while following the spiritual path, and I was interested to know whether Rijumati had faced any doubts at any stage in his path.

'Of course I have, although I had to face the biggest ones early on when I was first getting involved as a Buddhist, and I had to work through them in order to become fully committed. I do still have doubts as to whether I can really live up to the ideal as I understand it. I often fall short, for instance if someone is annoying me and I realize I can't even be compassionate to one person, let alone all those beings out there.... Yes, I have my doubts.

'But the quality of determination keeps me going, no matter how tough it is. One of my favourite science fiction movies is *Terminator 2*. There's a robot that's just unstoppable, made of liquid metal – he's completely pliable and can change into any form. Apart from the fact that he's trying to kill people – which is a bit of a downer from a Buddhist point of view – I find it a strong image: this determination that's completely flexible yet unstoppable.'

Another aspect of service is the collective side, working and cooperating with others who have the same vision, learning from one another, encouraging and supporting one another, and deriving spiritual benefits from one another. I wanted to know more about the day-to-day inspiration Rijumati gets from working with others.

'I've learned a tremendous amount from Vajraketu: his commitment to what he is doing for the business, and before that his work in India. Vajraketu sometimes used to say to me that commitment is freedom, and I used to think that he was just coercing me to stay at Windhorse because we were having manpower shortages. "I'm not having this!" I'd think. But once I'd got over my reactions, which took several years, I came to realize that by participating with others who share a collective vision, not only do you lay down the burden I've already talked about, but something magical happens. I've felt a strong sense of single-mindedness.

'For example, within the management team we're struggling towards something, and none of us knows entirely how to manifest it or quite what it is, but we share determination and energy. An idea pops up, and we don't really know whose idea it was. That shared vision on the basis of commitment to the ideals of Buddhism and what the FWBO has to offer has been a high point of working together here. The moments of one-mindedness in a spiritually committed group of friends give one great spiritual confidence in the practice of service. This is because we are all serving the Dharma together and we can directly experience the harmony and fellowship this creates, delighting in the mutual transformation of wills away from the self-orientated towards the other-orientated; from me, me, me, to altruism.

'It's obvious Vajraketu isn't doing this for his personal glory. There can't be many managing directors in the world whose only personal space is one small room, living on minimal pocket money, and happily sharing their life with all-comers, that is, with anyone who comes to work in Windhorse and shares in that vision. That ideal of brotherhood and sisterhood moves me very deeply. We're serving the Dharma together and that helps us to realize more than just our own vision of the Dharma. Within that I feel a fidelity and loyalty to those with whom I work. I wouldn't want to leave Vajraketu without my support while he still needed it.'

Rijumati and I talked about the book and film, *The Remains of the Day*, in which a butler devotes his life to Lord Darlington, who it turns out is a Nazi sympathizer. At the end of the film both the butler and the lord are lost causes. No one wants to know them. The butler has served selflessly, but has served something ignoble.

'One has to be discriminating, and these were some of my own tussles, although questions of power and exploitation have not been significant ones for me in the last seven or eight years. One positive image for me connected with service is disciple-ship. The good disciple is sincere in his or her practice, and in-telligent, asking all the time, "Is this ethical? Is this skilful?" I am quite prepared to criticize the behaviour of those who work in Windhorse, whether they are on the management team or new to the business. Sometimes this makes me unpopular, but unpop-ularity is far better than ethical compromise and collusion. One senior member of the business has told me I'm rather abrasive. I do try to put things in the best possible way and I'm much less of the bull in a china shop than I used to be.'

> **Unpopularity is far better than ethical compromise and collusion.**

Service is obviously connected with the depth of one's com-mitment. Some important ideas arose during a study seminar led for some men who had been working long-term in the busi-ness. Sangharakshita, who was leading the seminar, talked about something from the Christian monastic tradition of the middle ages: the vow of stability. The medieval monasteries faced some of the difficulties of rapid change that are common nowadays, for the monks and nuns had less responsibilities than most people. They were not tied to home and family, so they could move around. This caused a real problem. In some of the larger abbeys and monasteries there was a lot of change as they grew, and not enough mature and committed people stay-ing in one place to keep the spirit alive. So some monks took a vow of stability, which meant they commited themselves to a monastery for a number of years in order to help it to thrive.

'I've thought about this a lot in relation to Windhorse, and I aspire to be mature enough to make that commitment, although I'm not saying that it is life-long. I am happy to stay here as long as I have the sense that I am able to be effective and useful and not get in the way of letting other people take things on; and that I still feel that I'm spiritually evolving and making progress myself. While the answer to both these points is still in the affir-mative, I don't think of going anywhere else. It would be irre-sponsible to rock the boat while it is still proving effective.'

16

PROFIT OR PRINCIPLES?

WINDHORSE:EVOLUTION buys and sells, makes a profit and, hopefully, not too many losses. A question a lot of people ask – Buddhists and non-Buddhists alike – about running a giftware business is, 'Doesn't it encourage greed and consumerism, which are surely antithetical to a Buddhist world view?' Vajradarshini, whom we met in Chapter 1, has reflected long and hard on this question.

'It's just so easy to have a simplistic view. Consumerism is an attitude that is everywhere. You see it in any aspect of retail in a very obvious way. Some people might think, well, if you want to work in retail at least you could work in something more appropriate for a Buddhist, such as a wholefood shop, rather than selling giftware. But there's really just as much consumerism in the world of health foods. I went to a festival of Mind, Body, and Spirit a while ago, and it was awful in terms of the consumerism and neediness in people. Sad to say you even get consumerism in relation to spirituality, a grabbing and an appropriation. So I think it's too simplistic to say that working in a gift shop is encouraging greed but doing something else isn't. If I thought I could make more money to give away doing something else then I might do so, but I don't think the giftware business is a bad thing.

'And I have no problem about selling things that are useless: life isn't about being useful and practical and utilitarian. Also, people come in the shop and buy things I don't like, yet they obviously like them – I don't like sitting in judgement on someone else's taste. Almost always people buy our products as gifts for someone else, or sometimes as light-hearted treats for them-selves. I like the fact that we wrap the goods properly and put on one of our stickers, and people love our carrier bags. We *don't* get people in the shop who display particular neediness or craving; they can buy an attractive present for a friend, and get good value for money.

> You can't always have what you want, but you can always want what you have.

'However, I have to admit that it's hard being in the world of buying and selling and engaging in it fully without wanting to appropriate things. Working with that tension becomes a prac-tice in itself and a subject for a lot of reflection. My grandad used to say, "You can't always have what you want, but you can always want what you have."

'If I lived and worked in a retreat centre, I'd probably be happy to have an even simpler life than I do now. In the world of retail, I'm choosing to engage with what's happening in the world in the sense of who's doing what, what's fashionable, and who or what is influencing what. There's a whole world you can engage with if you want and you don't have to be greedy about it. I find it all very fascinating. For instance, I'm fascinated by what music people are listening to. What does it say about cur-rent values? How is society shifting, and what does all that mean to people practising the Dharma? How do we reach those people? I'm interested in the way these two worlds meet.

'Working in a gift shop frees up money to be used to spread the Dharma. Some people have put it to me that I would be better working in the caring professions, even suggesting I run a soup kitchen. While these things would be a very good form of livelihood for a Buddhist, I think it's even more important that people have the Dharma and that it's available for all. There are lots of people doing more obvious "social" work, whereas there are very few Buddhists who are happy to make money for the spread of the Dharma. A lot of Buddhists don't like the world of commerce. Because I'm quite happy doing it, it seems the best thing for me to do. I see money as something to be freed up for other possibilities to proceed.'

As far as we know, the Buddha said little about money and wealth. He certainly didn't say that money was an evil, nor advance poverty as a synonym for godliness. He taught merchants, royalty, labourers, and ascetics alike, not scorning any one lifestyle, though he did recognize that some lifestyles were more conducive to spiritual development than others. He encouraged his followers not to cling to worldliness, the operative word being 'cling'. Accumulation of personal assets, to which one might become attached, he saw as a hindrance to spiritual progress, but he didn't single out attachment to wealth as a greater evil than any other appetite leading to craving, such as intoxication for power and status, holding fixed views, or being obsessed by sexual desire. Poverty is not elevated as a state blessed in itself, though simplicity is. The great twentieth-century Indian leader, Dr B.R. Ambedkar – who led hundreds of thousands of his followers, from the lowest of the Indian castes, in their conversion to Buddhism, a man who had seen and experienced the worst excesses of poverty – made a statement about wealth that I have always found thought provoking: 'Renunciation of riches by those who have it may be a blessed state. But poverty never can be. To declare poverty to be a blessed state is to pervert religion, perpetuate vice crime, to consent to make earth a living hell.'[14]

In the *Sigālovāda Sutta* (*Dīgha Nikāya* 31) the Buddha gives sound business advice about the way a master should minister to his workers: by arranging their work according to their strengths, by supplying them with food and wages, by looking after them when they are ill, and by giving them time off when appropriate. Workers respond by performing their duties well and by protecting the good name and fame of their master. These basics still apply today. Vajradarshini spoke of a particularly illuminating realization she had about Right Livelihood business a few years ago.

'I went to a trade fair with Vajraketu. I was only 24 and I found it rather overwhelming. I encountered people of my own age who were buyers for large and well-known shops and department stores. I saw this young woman at one of the booths looking very smart with her briefcase, and she seemed to know her job inside out and was very professional. It struck me that I should be doing my job like that. Until then, I was under the illusion that it was OK not to do my job in a particularly professional way or fully engage in it, because it was just a means to an end, and as a Buddhist one shouldn't get too involved in the means. This woman's motivation was no doubt a combination of a good salary and seemingly an enjoyment of the task itself. And I thought, I should be doing the job even better! But I was a bit scruffy, almost as though that was the way Buddhists should present themselves. I thought, if I'm going to do this job, I have to engage with it fully, and enjoy it. I don't believe something can be a practice if you're not engaged. If you think working in an Evolution shop is just consumerism and you have an aversion to that, then it won't be a practice because you won't be able to engage. So one has to find ways of engaging with the shop as a shop. It may be through the goods, the way they're displayed and look of the place, or maybe through customer service and efficient business management. However we do it, to make it a practice we really have to engage with the nuts and bolts of running a shop.'

Talking to Vajraketu, the managing director, about money, profit, and business in general, I asked him about another, persistent criticism people used to raise about Windhorse in the early days: that those working in the business could bring in much more money for the FWBO by going out and getting regular jobs, rather than banding together for such low wages with such little return in profit. Vajraketu explains some of the reasons why they kept going.

'From the time I joined the business, we received a lot of criticism from within the FWBO. They were partly to do with the products we traded, which people thought tacky, but also because a lot of energy had been poured into the project but not much money was coming out the other end to give away. We reinvested our profits as a deliberate policy, rather than giving them away. It was Kulananda's way of building up the business, which I followed. So, for example, suppose early on we made £60,000 profit one year. If we had given away £40,000 of that, the following year we'd still only have made £60,000 profit. What we did was give away only £10,000 and keep £50,000 for reinvestment. The next year we'd make £100,000 and give away £30,000 and so on. Eventually we've come to a point now where we made £1.25m in 2001. Because we ploughed all that money back into the business at the beginning, we were able to give away £700,000 in 2001. If, on the other hand, back in 1989, we had given away two-thirds of the profits, today we would have a business that was only making a profit of perhaps £200,000.

'I once gave a public talk on Buddhist economics at an FWBO centre. A woman in the audience asked me what I thought was a reasonable amount of profit. I replied that I didn't have any notion of what was a reasonable profit – I'd sell something for what I thought I could get for it. She was clearly quite shocked and I could tell from the atmosphere in the audience that she was not alone. There was an underlying assumption in her question that there's a fair level of profit and anything above that is mildly indecent. I don't have that attitude myself.

'There's lots of controversy at the moment about AIDS drugs. If I was making huge profits from the drugs and there were millions of people dying from AIDS because the drugs were so expensive that people couldn't afford them, that would be different. But the goods we sell don't have any intrinsic moral worth, so I have no qualms about making as much profit as we can, as long as everyone gets a fair deal. I'll give an example. I'm offered an item by an artisan or supplier and it's someone I know, and let's say they ask £1 for it. Now I work to a certain extent on a formula for a selling price, so if I think I can get quite a bit more for it than the formula will produce on that £1 item then I offer them more for it. That means they too get more. I tend not to do this with manufactured goods made in Taiwan by a rich person. I haven't really articulated to myself a coherent economic theory to cover all this. There are elements of capitalism in it: we're out to make profit, and if we can make a bit more profit then we'll do so. Where we part company with capitalism is what we do with the profit: it is used for worthwhile purposes rather then for our own gratification. There would be some interesting work to be done to articulate a comprehensive theory of Buddhist economics.'

Reflecting on what Vajraketu has said, I don't believe there is a contradiction between Buddhism and business, as long as the business is run ethically, by which I mean that what is most important is the good intention behind the aims and actions of the company. Not all businesses would fit this category. Let's take the example of a multinational being threatened by a consumer boycott because of its exploitative employment model in the developing world. Imagine that, primarily responding to commercial pressure – on account of bad publicity received they are unable to sell their product – they improve their working conditions. Their publicity improves and the product sells once again. The working practices now in place might appear to be identical to another company that runs their business with a genuine feeling for humanity and a desire to participate in the betterment of society – as well as making a profit. The two companies might appear similar, but the working practices of the former have come about through fear and commerce, whereas those of the latter have arisen from humanitarian principles and ethics of intention. The latter is in accord with Buddhism, the former not.

Vajraketu continued, 'There is, however, a paradox at the heart of what we do. We have a vision of building a new society. It's taking a long time, but nevertheless there is this ideal. If we were to bring that new society about, it probably wouldn't need a business like ours. There are a few aesthetic pieces, but if everyone was living a life in accordance with the Dharma, you wouldn't really need to import soapstone carvings from Kenya. As it is, we're trying to build a new society within the old. And the new society both has to, and wishes to, make contact with the old one.

'If you were running a business that produced Dharma books, it wouldn't become obsolete, because you'd always need Dharma books. Whereas if Buddhism really did take a complete hold, it wouldn't need a giftware business like Windhorse:evolution. So we try to make as much profit as we can, in both the macro sense (the business as a whole) and the micro sense (on individual items), while trying to give everyone a good deal. I would understand and respect anyone who wanted to run a Right Livelihood business that was just involved with people and their spiritual development and wasn't concerned with making money. That would be a legitimate vision, as would be a Right Livelihood business that concentrated on the product, such as publishing Dharma books, or running a vegan restaurant. I'm sure one would like to make a profit selling Dharma books, but making a huge profit would be self-defeating. It would be better to sell the books cheaper and get more of them out into the world.

'I've been quite gratified that over the last six or seven years we have been making lots of money and putting that to good use. Buddhist centres have come into being through the money we have generated. I have benefited from Buddhism, so this gives me a way of putting something back. I live a lifestyle that is compatible with Buddhist practice and is very enjoyable. The tasks I perform are neither here nor there, but the context is richly meaningful. I can practise Buddhism and do it with others who have chosen to do the same.

'I don't think I was a natural businessman. But what I learned in some of my previous jobs was that if you anticipate the every need of a customer and do everything you can for them, it makes them happy and they give you lots of work because it makes their life easier.'

Later on, Vajraketu learned more about business from Kulananda, and then from his friend Allan Hilder, who first came across Windhorse at a trade show and subsequently loaned them money at a crucial time. 'I'd talk to Allan two or three times a week on the phone. He gave me lots of business advice. I had little idea what I was doing when I first took over the business; five or six years later I had a rough idea, and now there are a number of areas of the business where I feel quite confident. When I think back on all the money we borrowed, it's amazing that Windhorse survived. At one point we owed £750,000 and had made £40,000 that year. That was the scariest point: we owed twenty years' worth of profit. Our loans subsequently exceeded £1m, but by then we were making more money and it was less scary. I just assumed everything would work out in the end, and it did. There's an element of good fortune in that.'

Many people, Buddhists and non-Buddhists alike, seem to find an incongruity between being a Buddhist and being a businessman. In Chapter 1 Vajradarshini talked vigorously about this seeming anomaly while working in an Evolution shop in Norwich. Now Vajraketu gives his point of view.

'In the early years of the business I used to read biographies and autobiographies of successful businessmen. You see their books at airports. I read them not because I wanted information about how to read accounts and so forth, but because I wanted to imbibe the spirit of those people. If I wanted to be a successful businessman I had to think like one. The only way I could develop that ability was by reading books about people like Akio Morita the Japanese co-founder of Sony Corporation, John Sculley the American chief executive of Apple Computers, or Richard Branson the founder, president, and chairman of the Virgin group. When I read these books, it was like this was the Dharma. I didn't feel less of a Buddhist, nor that I was engaged in a less Buddhist activity than when I was reading the *Dhammapada* or a Mahāyāna *sūtra*. It wasn't as though I was treating those people as idols – I was reading them because a Bodhisattva "masters all Dharmas", that is, does whatever is necessary to execute his or her Bodhisattva work. It's similar to when I went to India and studied Marathi, a local language, so as to help me work there more effectively. If you want to make money for the FWBO, you become a good businessman. It's no good holding your nose and detaching yourself; you couldn't be a successful businessman and have a disdain for the act of business. I had to throw myself in fully. At the same time, I wasn't personally drawn to it, so it required a certain amount of effort.

'I'd also listen to the business news and read the business papers, imbibing the world of business. So I could meet another businessman or businesswoman and step into their world because I was keeping in touch with it. A Bodhisattva could do that and remain detached, but I had to find points of interest. I no longer read business books, they've ceased to function for me, but I do read the business pages and listen to business reports on the radio. Objectively I need to keep track of interest rates, the exchange rate, and so forth. The euro will affect our business significantly; I need to keep up with that and know what the issues are.'

Becoming a businessman wasn't just learning the ropes and imbibing the spirit, Vajraketu also felt the need to manifest it outwardly. 'A few years ago I always wore jeans to work, but at the same time I was trying to engage with myself as a Buddhist businessman. At some point I got stuck. The only thing I could think of was to wear a suit and tie. It worked! These days I always wear a suit and tie to work. At first I felt a wally, but gradually I started relating to myself more as a businessman. Now I feel quite comfortable in a suit.

'There are some secondary and tertiary benefits to running a giftware business that quite appeal to me. One is that it doesn't fit with people's stereotype of Buddhists. I'm very keen on things like vegetarian restaurants and wholefood shops, yet I also think it's good that we run a business that you wouldn't necessarily associate with Buddhists, because it brings you more into contact with the world. I have lots of dealings with bank managers, lawyers, property people, and so forth. And while this is not a reason for doing it, I see it as a positive spin-off that many people come into contact with living Buddhists through us. I think we usually create a positive impression and it goes some way towards undermining people's stereotypes. It's a small side benefit, but one that gives me great satisfaction. I know we have a very trusting relationship with our bank. On at least two or three occasions they have explicitly said that they've done something because they know they can trust us. So if we ring up and ask for an extension of our overdraft, and we give them a plausible reason, they believe us.

'The bank managers, lawyers, and so forth all know we are Buddhists. The information emerges naturally at an appropriate time. We used to fret a bit in the early days about whether and when should we tell them. We don't actively publicize it, although all our notepaper and so forth has on the bottom: "Windhorse Trading Ltd is a wholly owned subsidiary of the Windhorse Trust, registered charity no....", so at least anyone who receives our notepaper knows we're a charity.

'The fact that we're Buddhists emerges naturally as you get to know people. I would say all our customers know this, except a few that we see only once or twice at a trade show. We certainly don't go out of our way to bring it up in conversation. Incidentally, as with all Order members in the business, when dealing with non-Buddhist business colleagues we use our birth names. I don't find it odd being called Bob Jones within that context, although my Buddhist friends at work all call me Vajraketu.

'The questions I am asked, once people know we are Buddhists, are more along the lines of, "are you allowed to ..." this or that, rather than anything more substantial, but I don't think that stops them being fascinated. People such as the lawyers, auditors, and bank managers know of course that we don't pay ourselves very much, that the directors of the company pay themselves the same as everyone else, and they find that admirable. I sense that these people quite like the association. They probably like helping people who are doing something a bit different, though I don't suppose they are sentimental about it.'

One reason Vajraketu changed his life at a fairly young age was a recognition of the effect his lifestyle was having on him, moving from working firstly in the theatre and then from a classical music company to a more commercial way of life.

'I didn't have much self-awareness, but I did have a surprising insight into what is important in life around this time. I'd really enjoyed working in the classical record company. The people were good and I loved the product. The only thing wrong was that I didn't make much money. When I'd been in the theatre, I'd hung out with people who would take me to Covent Garden and go out to dinner afterwards. I thought I missed that lifestyle, so I got a job as a sales rep for a pop music company in order to earn money to do these things which I thought I missed. I started making a lot of money quickly, had a flat of my own, a car, and plenty of money to lead any sort of social life I wanted.

'But I realized one day that the very thing I wasn't doing was going to Covent Garden and dining out afterwards. What I was doing instead was going to cocktail lounges and clubs, because that was what the people I now worked with did. Basically I was coarsened by it. The insight I had was that I'd set out to make money with the intention of doing something relatively refined, but along the way I was changed by what I was doing. Whereas before I used to listen to classical music, I was now listening to rock music. I realized that the person I was becoming didn't fit with the person I thought I was, and the new person was actually coarser and less interesting than the person I thought I was or wanted to be! This was my insight, and I realized that the longer I did this, the wider the gap was going to be.

I now asked him whether there were still aspects of 'grubby' business that have a coarsening effect on him.

'It's on business trips abroad that I'm most aware of the coarsening effects. When I am in Cambridge, I work hard all day, and three times a week I go out for a long run alongside the river and then home to the community. I might be tired, so if I've an evening to myself I tend to relax by reading "quality" literature, or science or history, and probably listen to some classical music. But on business trips abroad there's much more of a temptation to turn on the TV in the hotel room. We don't have one in the community. The urge to watch TV at home is virtually absent, but after a long day at a trade show, while living in sterile hotels, the "red meat" of buying and selling has to some degree coarsened me and I want to watch TV. Now that the business is better off, I tend to stay in more upmarket hotels, with a gym, if possible. It's far better to spend a couple of hours in the gym rather than watching cruddy American movies. I attempt to keep up a meditation practice while abroad, and carry a small portable shrine with me that I can set up in the hotel room. I also travel with a CD player and some good books. That said, I still have to wrestle with temptations such as TV and shopping, and watch myself with varying degrees of success. There's no doubt I waste more time abroad than I'm happy with.'

Vajraketu's perspective obviously comes from his working in the business for many years, but how is it viewed from the outside? I wrote to Vajraketu's friend and business mentor from the early days of Windhorse, Allan Hilder, to ask if he'd be willing to write something about his impressions of the company, both back in the early 1980s and now. Here is his response.

'I first came across Windhorse at the International Spring Fair in Birmingham. I think it was in February 1983. At that time, I had my own small giftware importing business, the Green Tree Company. Like all exhibitors I walked around the show looking at what our competitors were doing, and I noticed a newcomer selling paper lampshades, which were our best selling product at the time. While the rest of us involved in the lampshade business went to great lengths to hang and illuminate the paper globes in order to show them to their best advantage, these new guys had simply tied a piece of string across the back wall and attached a number of shades to it. They weren't really hanging at all; they sort of projected off the wall.

'The second thing I noticed about this new company was that the salesmen understood little about the psychology of selling; they sat squarely in the middle of the stand surrounded by products on three sides, most of which was inaccessible to prospective buyers. It was the perfect way to deter buyers from stepping on to the stand. However, they had one great advantage over us, we who supposed ourselves to be hardened professionals. They smiled beatifically at all-comers, whereas we scowled, believing every visitor who expressed interest to be a potential spy. Smiling turns out to have been a good business strategy. Eight years later my company went into liquidation while the successors to the original naïve pair of salesmen have taken Windhorse to unimagined success.

'I approached these newcomers and they responded in a friendly manner, even when I announced that I was a competitor. I sent my two colleagues to have a look, much as one might send someone to look at strange animals in the zoo. And Birmingham was like a zoo. It turned out that these animals were exotic rather than strange. One of them, Kulananda, was outgoing; his partner, Dharmananda, more introvert. We spoke several times at the show and, over the coming months through long telephone conversations, came to understand one another and a friendship developed between us. I learned of the purpose of their venture and was both intrigued and interested. I came to act as a sounding board for Kulananda and a sort of ex-officio finance director for a short while. Some eighteen months after our original meeting, Kulananda and I devised a sort of marriage with benefits for both of our organizations. I could not see how they would succeed given the margins they were making selling goods imported by others. They needed to import direct from producers, but they had no experience and no finance. I wanted to get out of the gifts business to concentrate solely on lighting. The solution was simple. Windhorse bought all Green Tree's stock of gifts on credit and acquired our customer list, and I undertook to introduce Kulananda to our very limited range of suppliers in the Far East. I would also introduce the company to a possible source of import finance. It worked to our mutual advantage and provided me with very entertaining company – Kulananda and, later, Kuladitya – on trips to the Far East.

'One day, in 1985 I think, Kulananda told me that he had someone important he wanted me to meet. I travelled down from York to Bethnal Green especially for the meeting. The three of us were to have lunch at the Cherry Orchard vegetarian restaurant. The very important friend, a chap dressed in a three-piece pinstripe suit, was Vajraketu. Despite his dress sense (which, thankfully, soon improved) I was drawn to him and we got on very well. I was keen to continue my, albeit slight, involvement with Windhorse when Kulananda left to work elsewhere in the FWBO. Vajraketu and I developed a strong bond; we often travelled together and, because jointly we were spending so many nights in Taiwan, we decided to set up an office/apartment where we stayed while in Taipei city. Through my lighting contacts, I had come to know a charming Chinese guy, David Kuo, and proposed to Vajraketu that he become our joint representative. I am happy that David is still working with Windhorse some fifteen years later!

'The opening of a joint office in an open-ended arrangement is the sort of operation fraught with possible dangers. Both companies were to contribute half the running costs each month, but should one party pull out, there was no way legally to enforce this arrangement. What if one company decided that it was spending fewer nights in the apartment and wanted to pay less? What if they didn't have the cash flow or lost interest? There is only one company with whom I would have considered entering into such an arrangement: Windhorse:evolution. The reason is that I had, and still have, absolute trust in the integrity of the people involved.

'Because of our personalities and the chemistry between us, I had enjoyed a bouncy and hectic relationship with Kulananda, largely conducted via long telephone conversations. My relationship with Vajraketu has been founded on more solid ground, but has been no less fun. I had a strong sense in the beginning of being "handed over" to Vajraketu, and that alone might have caused our relationship to be stillborn. However, over the years we have met regularly and made time for one another, spending days or evenings at regular summit meetings in "inspiring and spiritually healing" places such as Peterborough. My brief and early contribution to Windhorse as stand-in finance director has been more than amply repaid by Vajraketu's dedicated guidance on morality. Whenever I have considered any mildly devious business scheme I have run it past Vajraketu. If he is shocked I don't do it. If he greets it with only mild disapproval I'm certain it is perfectly ethical!

'As an outsider with some familiarity of the workings of Windhorse, I have developed a great respect and admiration for the organization. These feelings are based not only on its economic success, but also for the way in which that success has been achieved. I have been particularly fascinated by the importance of the individual within the structure, and the way that the political and personal tensions found in any organization are resolved within Windhorse: not through internal conflict but through going for long walks. This has seemed to me admirable and beautifully eccentric. I am quite certain that Windhorse's success is due to the fact that everyone is working for a common goal and takes seriously their responsibilities within the framework of achieving that goal, as well as spending half their working day walking along the riverbank.

'I am well aware that keeping such an ostensibly ego-free ship on course is not easy and demands constant attention. I believe that the company has benefited from excellent leadership and, in particular, from a real understanding of what individuals concerned in such a joint enterprise need to maintain their motivation.

'I have occasionally wondered why Windhorse has continued to prosper when, in bad times, competitors have failed. Good buying and diversity of operations I'm sure have been factors, but I suspect customer loyalty has also played a part. As a former retailer, I know I felt positively about certain suppliers and negatively about others. This was based on a load of factors, including how the company treated me. While I would not necessarily have favoured Windhorse because its aims were charitable, or because it was a Buddhist organization, I would have favoured any company that consistently treated me with respect. I think, in this way, the Buddhist principles underlying the involvement of the people at Windhorse have contributed in no small way to its economic success.

'One final point. I am amazed that a *Telegraph* reader who loves peace and tea as Vajraketu does, and who is loathe to bathe in brash alien cultures (Chinese neon) has managed to keep going for so long on Far East buying trips!'

Roy Marriott

Satyaloka: Working at
Windhorse 'was not all
sweetness and light'

Cambridge Evolution Shop

The Windhorse:evolution team
in front of their old premises

Leaving to get ordained

17

GLOBAL CONNECTIONS

AS A CONSEQUENCE of Windhorse:evolution's trade in giftware, the business and its workers are connected to people and companies from around the world. Buddhism teaches that all actions have consequences, and in this chapter I want to look at the impact of this trade. It is a complex area because the world is a complex place. It is impossible to be black and white in the moral maze that it involves, but we can tend to a lighter shade of grey, and try to be as ethical as we can. I'll describe how our business benefits people around the world who produce the goods we sell, and I'll also explore some of the ethical issues that arise and how we respond to them.

The buying I have most enjoyed involves dealing directly with producers in their countries of origin, where I can witness at first hand how the products are crafted and under what conditions. It can be very gratifying to see that we have a substantial effect on the local economy. One particularly heart-warming liaison of ours is with soapstone carvers in Kenya.

Pauline Ntombara is a Kenyan woman who lives with her family in Cambridge. They came to England ten years ago. Her husband is a Methodist minister studying development economics. As well as generating some income for her family, Pauline helps to further her husband's studies and give their two children what she describes as a far better education than would be possible in Kenya. They intend to stay in Cambridge until the children have finished school, and then return to Kenya.

Nine years ago, Pauline came into our shop with a carrier bag filled with a few soapstone artefacts wrapped in newspaper, and asked whether we would be interested in selling them. At the time, the shop still did some of its own buying, especially when we thought it would help local people. The carvings sold. We bought more. We put Pauline on to our central buyers, and thus started a very productive relationship. She mobilized the people she knew in Kenya to make the goods we wanted from the samples she showed us. Over the last six years, a lot of soapstone has been sold through Evolution shops and off the vans, and it is now beautifying the sitting rooms of many English homes.

In early 2000 we took up Pauline's oft-repeated invitation to visit Kenya to further develop the work we were doing together. Vajraketu and I spent our first few days with Pauline in the markets of Nairobi, mainly collecting woodcarvings. She priced them up in consultation with the woodcarvers, and laid the items out in a room in the Methodist guesthouse. There we spent a day sifting through the samples, selecting those we particularly liked, and sometimes negotiating prices. Our policy, wherever we do business, is to accept the asking price if we think that, with our usual mark-up, we can sell the product fairly easily. We don't try to make a bit extra by pushing the suppliers on price. By that evening, we had placed orders totalling about £60,000. I particularly liked the items we bought, which helps engagement enormously. Pauline was pleased we were satisfied enough to make a sizeable order, the woodcarvers were thrilled to have the work, and the head of the guesthouse was delighted with Pauline's initiative, because it provided employment for many people.

From Nairobi we went out to villages about two hours' drive away to buy colourful baskets from a women's cooperative. This enterprise had been established by a Scandinavian charity, and though we met one Norwegian man, all our negotiations were done through the local Kenyan women. We saw the women walking up and down the dusty lanes, chatting with each other while weaving baskets. Pauline particularly enjoys seeing women finding employment. She tells me there is a lot of drinking among the men, so hard-earned money is often frittered away while the children have to go without food and education. With the finances in the hands of the women, money can be spent more wisely. We made a conservative order of baskets, which looked very good in our shops when they were unpacked six months later. Pauline dealt with all the packing and shipping of the goods. She has competent helpers who do much of the work while she is in England, but she makes several visits to Kenya each year herself to help the movement of orders, quality control, and so forth run as smoothly as possible. Considering from what small beginnings we started working with her, I was much impressed by the organization she had in place.

A jeep ride of many hours along the worst roads I have ever experienced (and I have done a lot of travelling in my time, in many countries) brought us to the bustling town of Kisii, some fifty miles south of the equator. Even where there was a notion of tarmac, the potholes were so deep and so frequent that we rarely travelled more than 30 mph. We constantly swerved from one side of the road to the other to avoid them. Light relief was, however, provided by the beautiful and surprisingly lush countryside, the deep blue cloudless skies, in some areas the colourful Masai tribal people at the roadside, and from the good nature and careful negotiations of our driver, who was Pauline's nephew, Gitari. A further forty-minute drive up steep red-dust roads resembling dried-up river beds brought us to the village of Tabaka, where the soapstone is sculpted, then carved and etched, into designs that are saleable in the West.

Nearby are the soapstone quarries. Large chunks of the stone are transported to a huddle of buildings and open spaces covered with corrugated-iron roofs. The men do the sculpting with the most primitive of saws, axes, chisels, and files, sitting on the ground in the shade. There are no tables or benches, and no electricity in the work areas, so no powered tools. Generations of the people in Tabaka have learned this craft which, apart from farming, is their only source of income. Once a rough model is made, the women take over, sanding down the carvings with ever-finer degrees of sandpaper and washing them in buckets of water. Again they sit together in groups under a metal canopy, or a tree, or in the doorways of their basic mud huts. After the sanding comes the polishing, again by the women.

Shortly after arriving, and a much-needed wash, we spent the afternoon going around the numerous 'showrooms' in the village, picking up possible samples. The showrooms were wood and mud huts about ten feet square piled high with soapstone artefacts. Pauline is one of many people who deal in soapstone. Apparently foreigners come to the village from all over the world to buy it, though it is hard to imagine many of them making the arduous journey, and we certainly never saw another white face. However, it seems that Pauline is one of the biggest mobilizers and consolidators, and we discovered she was at that time providing work for more than 400 people in the area. She is a Christian. As far as I am aware, all her workers are Christians, a combination of Methodists, Roman Catholics, and Seventh Day Adventists. The unity and zeal of those communities seems to hold the whole thing together. As an aside, during the years I worked in India I noticed that it was nearly always the Christian community who were doing the most impressive social work. Buddhists, I feel, still have a lot to learn from them in this area.

We spent much of the next three days in the small rooms where we also slept. We went through the samples we had picked up, and further samples based on our own designs arrived in quick succession. The designs came from magazine photos, sketches by our own talented young designer, Victoria, and quite a lot of on-the-spot development of ideas. It was fascinating to watch the forms develop before our eyes. We looked at abstract Henry Moore-like sculptures, elephant bookends, dancing women, intricate boxes, and spiral candlesticks, to name but a few. In the hours before we left, a number of sculptors stayed up all night under a single electric light bulb to complete further samples. Throughout the star-spangled night I could hear the faint tap-tapping of metal on stone, and the rub-rubbing of sandpaper with the slosh of water. Some of the designs worked and some didn't, but we ended up placing an order worth £80,000. Everyone was delighted. To have new designs was a challenge for them and made them very happy, and the size of the order meant work for all for many months to come.

Pauline is well aware of the possible dependency on our continuing trade with Tabaka. Soapstone sells well now in England but, like any other product, if the fashion wanes we will not be able to continue buying it. She has other customers in Europe and America, and has started showing her products at trade shows abroad, so as not to be solely dependent on us. However, it is through us that she has built up the infrastructure that enables her to do this. This last Christmas period back in England saw a high turnover in sales of the soapstone, which I found very gratifying. When wrapping such a sculpture in tissue paper at the counter of our Cambridge shop, my mind briefly reverts to those families in Kisii.

If it had not been for a passing comment from Pauline, we might never have known that we had been indirectly partially responsible for the construction of a large primary school in the area to accommodate 600 children. A while ago, Pauline led a *harambee* (a term coined by Jomo Kenyatta that means 'pulling together', suggesting something like teamwork) in the locality. They needed money for a primary school for children from all tribes and religious persuasions. The village leaders and elders looked at ways to raise the money. Pauline decided to put half her profits towards the school and, inspired by her, the carvers also donated money, giving between them two-thirds of the cost of the simple school building, which is now in use. I was deeply impressed both that they were interested in helping the community beyond their own needs, and also that their wages were clearly enough to be able to give something away.

I have just returned from a subsequent visit to buy more soapstone and develop new designs, taking a friend who works in accounts as a companion. Maitridevi is much hotter on environmental issues than me. I was interested to see what she would make of the soapstone operation. From an environmental point of view, it seems evidently silly, she said, to ship large quantities of extremely heavy, non-utilitarian items 5,000 km for the sake of consumers in the UK. But once she had met the people, who now have enough money to feed, clothe, house, and educate themselves, she saw things in a different light. She even began to feel the developed world had a duty to buy from the developing world, if that is what it takes to give people employment and a decent income.

Fair Trade is often discussed in our particular line of work, and all those working in Windhorse:evolution, and many of our customers, are concerned about it. Fair Trade means different things to different people – there is no absolute standard of what constitutes it, but the basic principles are clear: the producers get a fair share of the proceeds of any trade, as opposed to a situation where the arrangement is stacked heavily in favour of the buyer or the employer. In addition, there is an assumption that labour is given freely (no bonded labour or forced child labour), and that working conditions are safe and humane. There is also usually an assumption that goods are produced in an environmentally friendly way.

When Windhorse first began, all our goods were bought from other wholesalers in the UK and mainland Europe, and we had almost no idea of the circumstances under which they were produced. This was progressively replaced by direct buying at trade shows in the Far East, mainly in Taiwan. During that phase we started to visit some of the places where the products were actually made.

In recent years we have been steadily increasing the proportion of our goods from places we can visit and where we can get into a creative relationship with the manufacturers. A strict Fair Trade company would visit every production source before buying, and though we are moving in that direction, we have not arrived there yet. So we cannot claim we are a fully 'Fair Trading' company, though much of the way we trade will certainly overlap, as illustrated by our trade with Kenya. Some of our ethical concerns, however, differ from what is normally called Fair Trade. For example, we make sure we do not supply any goods containing animal products, such as leather, seashell, feathers, or animal resin, even if they were to be made by legitimate Fair Trade producers. We would not buy leather goods, no matter how 'fair' the conditions in which they were produced, because that would involve slaughtering animals, even if that trade might help the producers economically. After all, the gifts we sell are hardly necessities, and blatantly to destroy life for our home comforts seems distasteful.

I have to confess that sometimes at Windhorse we can be a little slow to realize the effects of our actions. An example of this occurred three years ago, when our best-selling items were inflatable plastic chairs from Taiwan. They were a big money-spinner, and that year the Evolution shops had their most profitable year to date, mainly due to sales of these items. However, the people in many of our shops didn't want to sell them because of environmental concerns over the amount of plastic involved. We were a little slow on the uptake, even perhaps slightly blinkered by the profits, but when stocks ran out we refrained from re-ordering them, even though customers were still asking for them two years later and we could have made considerably more profit.

We visit many countries, mostly in the Far East, to buy our merchandise. From some countries, such as Taiwan, we buy mostly mass-produced goods. In others we move more in the arena of handicrafts. I have made a number of buying trips to Bali and particularly enjoy meeting the family-based businesses from which we purchase many of our products. It is from them that we buy, among other things, a range of wooden artefacts that are carved from softwood from managed forests. In this instance, it is easy to be quite clear about the sourcing of the wood, because we have such a good relationship with the suppliers, and they are well-informed about environmental issues and our particular stance. If we were to discover environmental damage had occurred as a result of our purchases, we would move to alter our buying patterns (although we cannot pretend there is no environmental impact in transporting goods around the world). I mention woodcarvings because over the last eight years or so we have sold many varieties, from traditional masks and figures to items developed for Western tastes. As well as

concern about the materials used, we also take note of the conditions and surroundings in which the products are made. Naturally we would not buy from a sweatshop.

It is interesting to follow the production of a woodcarving and
see the various stages of labour and the cooperation among the
workforce. Let me use the example of a 'cute' cat, one of a pleth-
ora of such items that never go out of fashion. He is a cat with a
cheesy smile curled up asleep as though beside a log fire and
seems to draw out the exclamation, 'Ahh! isn't he sweet/cute/
gorgeous,' or, 'Doesn't he remind you of Marmalade, Oscar,
Tibbs, Felix?' An extended family in a Balinese village carves the
wood and puts it out to dry. Particular hill villages will often
specialize in and be characterized by one product or variation
thereof. Sometimes the whole production takes place within
one household, sometimes the carving is done in one place and
then taken to another household for painting and varnishing.
Households in the village share out the work and when it is
ready our consolidators, P.T.S., collect the cats by jeep and take
them to their warehouse where they are picked over for quality
control, wrapped, packed in boxes, and shipped to us.

Some people in the West want a guarantee that there is no
child labour attached to any of our products. We cannot give
such a guarantee. In fact I will go so far as to say that such a
guarantee could involve doing more harm than good. Because
businesses in Bali are family-based, there is a tendency for the
whole extended family to help with production: grandmother,
grandfather, mother, father, and cousins share out the carving,
sanding, painting, and varnishing. Although the men do most
of the carving, the business negotiations are as often managed
by women as by men. If you visit at weekends, or in the afternoon after school, there are frequently children helping with
the production too, mostly in the charming courtyards of their
family homes, sometimes gathered around a shrine dedicated

to the local deity. On a number of occasions I have visited work-shops opening out into the paddy fields or lush jungle where a child might be painting the whiskers of a cat or rubbing it with furniture polish while chatting and laughing with friends and siblings. Far from being exploitative, it is hard to imagine a healthier upbringing. All the children go to school, they wear shoes and neat clothing, and I have never seen a malnourished child there. Most will follow the trade of their forefathers and they tend to develop their skills while young. So the cute wooden cat that now sits on the corner of your bookshelf in your London flat, reminding you of Felix, might possibly have had a Balinese child's touch to it.

The whole question of child labour is a complex and emotive one, and I was interested and actually heartened when talking to representatives of a large UK-based charity that promotes Fair Trading to find that, like me, they could not be as categorical on these issues as most Westerners would like them to be.

In Bali it is fairly straightforward to know where we stand on ethical and environmental issues. We have been dealing with some of these craftsmen and craftswomen for years and built up good working relationships with both the individual families and with our consolidators, who know the ethical stance we take. P.T.S. have built themselves up from a handful of workers to a significant support business for many local people, mainly through the trade we are able to offer them. Nowadays, not only do we buy traditional crafts plus their own innovations, we also give them our own designs for such things as mosaic mirrors, varieties of bamboo and metal windchimes, mobiles, novelty picture frames, and much more which they now make in their own workshops.

As well as Bali, we visit our producers in Kenya and Thailand, where it is easy to see at first hand the conditions in which people work, and the positive impact this income has on them.

India, on the other hand, is not quite so easy to assess. Because India is so vast, we are unable to visit all the factories in which our products are made. At first we have to rely entirely on the suppliers we meet at trade shows around the world. We have to assess, as far as practically possible, whether the company is represented by socially-aware people. The trading companies we deal with in India develop and market products, but sub-contract the actual production. We might buy several products from one company, but only visit the factories involved if the products or ranges are going to be re-ordered several times. In this area we fall short of what an overtly Fair Trading company would do.

About twenty per cent of our products come from China. This is perhaps the ethically most controversial aspect of our trading. For a start, most of the people who work in our chain of shops are Buddhist, and they are particularly sensitive to the treatment of their fellow Buddhists in Tibet. We consulted the Tibetan government in exile and were told that the Dalai Lama's policy is that the Tibetan people's argument is with the Chinese Government, not the Chinese people. Sanctions hurt the Chinese people, not the Government, so they are not in favour of sanctions. We therefore continue to trade with China.

In addition to concerns about Tibet, other ethical issues arise when dealing with China. Their rapid economic growth, particularly within the Special Economic Zones where our products are made, has led to the migration of thousands of people from all over the country. Many of them live in dormitories attached to the factories. They are drawn by wages up to twenty times what they can earn in rural China.

This presents any ethical person with a dilemma. On the one hand one would wish to have nothing to do with a system that involves thousands of people moving away from their homes just to produce things for Western consumers; on the other hand, the people move to these factories because they want a better life for their families: they want to send money to feed and educate their children, and it wouldn't help to refuse to trade with them.

On balance, we believe the positives of dealing with China outweigh the negatives, though we accept that those negatives are considerable. For us, the shade of grey in dealing with China is a bit darker than with most of the other countries where we do business.

Over the years we have seen a steady improvement in the positive ethical dimension of our buying and we are fairly convinced from our visits that the pay and benefits available to those involved in manufacturing our products are as good as the local average, and often much better. In addition, our trading partners in Bali provide free medical care on site for all their staff, and – along with one of our Indian suppliers and Pauline, our Kenyan supplier – they support investment in local community infrastructure from their profits.

As Buddhists, we have guiding principles and precepts that encourage harmony, honesty, and non-exploitation, and we have a vision for a better world.

We have ourselves recently decided to invest some of our profits in local community projects in the poorest areas where we do business, for example in Kenya, Thailand, and Vietnam. Money has been set aside and at the time of writing we are discussing with our local contacts the best way to invest in some of the communities with whom we trade, for example by supporting reforestation in northern Thailand, or helping the school in Tabaka.

I see this as a gratifying side effect rather than the main thrust of what we are doing. Our trading can never be totally 'pure', if only because we are involved in the whole ambivalent world of consumer goods, which has to be tainted however ethical the means of production. But the benefits of our work have to outweigh the grey areas in which we might find ourselves. As Buddhists, we have guiding principles and precepts that encourage harmony, honesty, and non-exploitation, and we have a vision for a better world. We consider that money is energy, and our profit can be used for tremendous good in the world. While trying to maximize this profit, we also wish to ensure that we interact with the world in accordance with our principles, and this needs our constant attention.

18

COMMUNITY LIFE

WINDHORSE:EVOLUTION comprises a community of Buddhist men and women engaged in a communal endeavour. Every individual is part of a team. There are many teams, each with their own communal endeavours and tasks, but intrinsically linked to one another. Collectively, these teams make up the whole of Windhorse:evolution. But the business does not exist in isolation. This particular team-based Right Livelihood endeavour is an integral part of the broader community of the FWBO, and that in turn is part of the worldwide Buddhist community of all those making the ideals and practices of Buddhism central to their lives. I want to spell this out because although the business is experimenting with a particular approach to Buddhist practice within a particular Buddhist community, it is not isolated from the global Buddhist community.

Of course the Buddha lived a rather different lifestyle from ours. He went from the luxury of his palaces to the forest, where he concerned himself with nothing but discovering the truth. His full awakening happened while he was alone in the forest. After his Enlightenment, he often spent time on his own or with a companion. At other times he would get together with a group of other wanderers. There also grew up around him a body of men and women who listened to his teachings and supported him by providing food and shelter. So it was that his disciples fell into two groups, the forest renunciants and the lay supporters, and there was a strong relationship between them. His message to all was 'Seek the truth.' He encouraged his disciples to give up worldliness, at the same time stressing that the Dharma was for everyone. Lifestyle was secondary to the commitment to discovering the truth, and the Buddha taught people from all walks of life.

Only after the passing away of the Buddha were there settled monastics, intermediate between the forest dwellers and the village and townsfolk. The true forest renunciants would spend all their time in the forest, whereas some monks – and, later, nuns – would base themselves just outside towns and villages, and these groups developed into monasteries. It was these settled monastics who helped to keep Buddhism as one tradition, and became an effective missionary force, spending much of their time preserving the Buddha's teachings in writing. Each section of this threefold model of Buddhist lifestyle needed the others to help it remain spiritually alert, for there were drawbacks and dangers within each. The Buddhist scriptures make it clear that Enlightenment was possible within all three lifestyles: householders, monks and nuns in monasteries, and homeless renunciants.

In Asia there has been a strong tradition of the laity financially and practically supporting those who are practising as monastics and forest renunciants. In the West this tradition is nowhere near as well established, so only a very limited number of serious Buddhist practitioners are supported in this way. In the West, therefore, we don't usually fit exclusively into one or other of the laity/renunciant/monastic categories and there is a great deal more overlap between them. For example, people raising families go on retreats, and people living in retreat centres spend some time with their families or partners, and stay in contact by phone, email, and letter. Serious Dharma practitioners often work in the world to support themselves while they practise. Windhorse:evolution does not fit neatly into any of the traditional categories either, so we use the term semi-monastic to describe our approach to practice: 'semi' because very few of us have chosen a celibate life or have fully renounced personal possessions. On the other hand, we put a lot of emphasis on communal practice, communal living in same-sex residential spiritual communities, working in same-sex teams, and participating in many collective activities such as the ritual I mentioned in Chapter 6. All these have a monastic flavour to them.

Undertaking the practice of Right Livelihood does not itself imply that one has also to live in a residential spiritual community. Indeed, not everyone who works in the business does so. Some people choose not to, while others are unable to due to personal circumstances. However, particularly in Cambridge, where the largest number of people in the business work together, we see living together in residential communities as an important complement to our approach to the practice of Right Livelihood. It is hard for individuals to maintain an edge to their spiritual practice, and it is also hard for groups of individuals to maintain their collective edge. We don't have to look far back in history to see radical initiatives such as the Co-operative Society and the Rowntree Foundation becoming gradually less and less distinguishable from ordinary businesses. In Windhorse:evolution we rely on creating, maintaining, and constantly deepening our connections and friendships with one another to support our individual and collective practice. We've found that an important way of doing this is to live together in residential spiritual communities. By the majority of us living as well as working together we can create an intense field of practice and a network of friendships that operates all day, every day. It benefits those who live in the residential communities and those who don't, helping us all to stay true to the radical vision of the business.

I now want to re-introduce Vijayamala, 'garland of victories', to speak about her path as a Buddhist. She describes various situations she has lived in, and says why she feels that living in a residential community is important for her and the many people with whom she has lived over the years. She has lived in a number of different environments: with her parents, 'playing house' with her boyfriend, college campus, a spell in a bedsit, and her first Buddhist community in Brighton. In India she had lived with her Buddhist brother Lokamitra and his Indian wife and baby, so that was an extended-family experience. On returning to Cambridge she once again lived on her own while studying accountancy, until her new Buddhist boyfriend, Jyotipala, moved in with her.

'He and I were very much a "Buddhist couple". We'd talk a lot about the Dharma while also having a lot of fun together. He did all the housework and kept me human while I was doing my course! Nevertheless I found it limiting. It's difficult to say exactly why, but there was something about all my energy going in one direction that wasn't meaningful enough, or broad enough. Although I loved him very much and was happy to be involved with him, and grew up a lot through that relationship, living together in that way felt limited because it didn't have any relevance to anyone but us.'

After two years of coupledom, having finished her accountancy course and working as our accountant, Vijayamala moved into a community again. 'I hadn't lived in a community for a long time and at first I was unhappy because I missed the intimate daily contact with Jyotipala, although we remained in a relationship for quite a while after that. I remember coming down to breakfast feeling heavy and sad – not really knowing how to relate to others in the community. Dhiranandi, who had moved from the north of England to be in Cambridge because she wanted to work in the Evolution shop, was able to cut through that unhappiness and relate to me, and I'm very grateful for that. She was a very good friend and got me through this patch. Gradually my world started to expand. By moving into the community I was going on my intuition, but the emotions took time to catch up.

'Until Dhiranandi moved in, none of the others in the community worked in Windhorse, and that was interesting from the community's point of view, for I think we needed different things. For those who didn't work in the business, the community was the main focus of their collective practice, whereas for us who did, it was more balanced between work and community. We'd go to work and might have quite an extensive reporting-in session with the work team, so that need was met. But the people who hadn't been working together would come home and want to explore their day and how they'd been working.'

After a year or so, during which time Vijayamala was ordained, more women working in the accounts team and the Cambridge shop wanted to live in a community, so Dhiranandi and Vijayamala started up a new community along with three other women and me. We wanted to provide the opportunity for women to work and live together.

'That started my Windhorse community "career". Sometimes I talk about it in terms of a job – not in the sense that you have to do it and you get paid for it – but living in communities is part of how I help people.'

Within two years, the women's wing of the business in Cambridge had evolved to a point at which yet more women wanted to join a community. At first those of us already living together were somewhat resistant to change because we were happy together, but in the end we decided it was best to set up a second women's community. Subsequently, Vijayamala has lived in four different communities, always being the pioneering one and helping to set them up, because of the need to house the growing numbers of women wanting to live communally, women who now came from all over the world.

'I've gained a lot from living and working with people, for it leaves no stone unturned. It has been powerful living as well as working together, and I believe it is what has moved me on most in my spiritual life. Of course, I could tell others to set up a community themselves, but I have gained a lot from living and working with more experienced people myself, so I was happy to help. It felt like quite a growing up for me, realizing that I can give in this way. It is a very simple thing to offer people; all I needed was an openness to share myself. I don't have to do anything in particular with the others, just be there with them, and that alone seems to be very effective.'

Vijayamala is about to move into her fifth Windhorse community, so I asked her how she felt.

'I'm sad at leave my old community and my friends there, but I have established a sense of connection with them and I'm moving on to connect with more people. Living together is different from how I see people at work. We share different aspects of our lives. Community living is a delicate balance: people want continuity and to go deeper, and I'm sympathetic towards that. But from experience I also seem to be able to move on into the next community and feel I have sustained my connections. It's like a growing organism, and you have to judge when the time is right to divide and expand. It's often quite a growthful time for people when a more experienced person moves out of their community and they have to step into their shoes.'

There was a time when, for logistical reasons, people joined the business in Cambridge but were not always able to move straight into a community. If they had arrived from overseas, we would find temporary accommodation for them. However, we have noticed that form some their arrival has not been as smooth as for people who were able to move straight into a community. Nowadays we do what we can to make it possible for people to move straight in with others who are already used to communal living. The men in the business have managed to achieve this dual living and working together since the business first moved to Cambridge. It has been a slower, more organic process for the women, and is still under review.

'Although I am quite garrulous and like talking to people, I think in many ways I connect more deeply with people when I am doing something or just hanging out with them rather than talking about ourselves. That's probably partly why I am attracted to team-based Right Livelihood, where there is a very strong common project, and community life is a part of that. I get a lot of emotional satisfaction from living and working with people. I wouldn't myself want to do the collective work without the community, nor could I imagine now living communally but not working together! Having said that, I've never been in a position where I've lived and worked with exactly the same people. At present I live with people from the accounts team, retail team, and shop team, yet we are all involved in the same overall project, but one woman I live with works elsewhere.

'Because I'm the person who has been in my office the longest, as well as relating to me as finance director, people very often look to me for other things at work, whereas in the community I'm just living with people. They don't have to look to me for anything specific. If I don't wash up, somebody else has to wash up; if they don't wash up, I have to. It's much more

even. In the community, if I don't hang out the washing someone else has got to do it, and who's going to tell me that I
shouldn't leave the lid off the toothpaste? These are very basic,
personal things that might be done according to roles in a family. In the community, the aim is to move into more creative relationships, where we can really share and appreciate each
other's qualities, and thereby go beyond ourselves. Ideally, the
members of a community need to be there for each other with a
good level of intimacy, be able to rely on each other, and have a
strong sense of what is going on in each other's lives.'

Although there are many different ways of living together in
communities, what we have found to work best so far in Cambridge is a routine in which we
meditate together in the mornings and eat together in the evenings. We share money for food,
shop communally for the household, and cook for each other on
a rota. Most communities also
have one evening a week which
the members spend together.

> The aim is to move into
> more creative
> relationships, where we
> can really share and
> appreciate each other's
> qualities, and thereby go
> beyond ourselves.

This time is spent in whatever way the community wishes –
which could be studying together, going to a film, concert, or
play, talking about our lives, performing rituals, celebrating
birthdays, playing games, writing poetry, or just hanging out
together. On other evenings and at weekends people do as they
please.

Our residential communities are either for men or for women,
rather than mixed, and members of the opposite sex are not
usually allowed in, except perhaps tradesmen or visiting parents. We have chosen to set things up in this way because we've
found it helpful in our practice of developing as individuals.
Our gender conditioning inevitably has a huge influence in our

lives. Paradoxically, we've found that living and working with members of our own sex helps us to develop more fully as human beings, and allows there to be less emphasis on our conscious and unconscious roles as men and women.

I ask Vijayamala if she had now found the meaning and connectedness for which she was searching in her youth. 'I feel there is meaning to my life when I am doing something of value, whether raising money for the FWBO or creating a context in which other Buddhists can live or work. As to connectedness, I am pushing forty and seem to have less of a drive to have an intense one-to-one relationship than I used to. I live with some younger women, and for some of them there are still these questions about wanting a deeper connectedness and seeing that in terms of having it with just one person. I've wondered why this is changing with me, for I don't feel less emotionally alive. On the contrary, I feel more emotionally alive, and more satisfied with my contact with people, than ever.'

When we choose to get involved with a broad spiritual community such as the FWBO we do so in order to change. To do this we need to be in regular, personal, and substantial contact with others who are also trying to develop as individuals whom we think will help us to develop. There are many ways for that contact to be developed – by no means does everyone *have* to work in a Right Livelihood business or live in a residential spiritual community. However, everyone needs to find the surroundings and circumstances within which genuine communication can develop in an effective, ongoing way. We need to participate in a supportive atmosphere where there can be real, even challenging, communication and a genuine spiritual exchange. Clearly, living together under one roof, and choosing that lifestyle in order to practise communication and awareness, is potentially such a context. Residential communities can be a very supportive environment, enhancing spiritual practice and psychological and spiritual growth.

There are also secondary benefits of communal living, and I would like to mention some of these before concluding this chapter. Broadly speaking, I see the secondary benefits as saving money (it is cheaper to live collectively) and reducing our environmental impact.

Several people living together can share resources, and several communities in close proximity can share even more. Here in Cambridge one lawn mower is shared between seven neighbouring communities and we have shared decorating and maintenance equipment. Choosing as we do to live simply, we cannot afford to buy lots of packaged and processed foods. We buy wholefoods and eco-friendly cleaning products in bulk at the warehouse, which the communities get at cost price. Some communities phone their fruit and veg orders through to a local greengrocer twice a week which is all included in a single delivery that arrives at the warehouse, including everything needed for the communal daily lunch. The greengrocery and wholefoods are then taken home on the usual daily shared transport between the warehouse and the communities. Bulk buying in this way not only makes economic sense but means there is less transportation and packaging and therefore less waste.

On the subject of transport, there are six cars for business use at the warehouse. Not even the managing director has his own car, although there is one that is kept for more official business visits and is therefore restricted to a few drivers to maximize its life as a smart car. In the evenings and at weekends the other five cars are available to anyone in the business who holds a licence. Our car park always looks very empty compared to those of the warehouses next door, even though we have considerably more people working in ours. We also own two minibuses which are used to ferry those people who don't bike into work between the warehouse and the communities every day. When a number of people are going to the same retreat we try to share transport either in the cars or the minibuses. We are also trying to develop ecological practice in other areas, and recently signed a contract with Ecotricity who supply electricity from renewable resources.

The simple, communal life has other benefits for the environment, direct and indirect. By living together we have more shared space and less personal space, and therefore need fewer personal possessions. There is a great tendency in our society to buy things we think we need and from which we assume we will gain pleasure and satisfaction. For those of us who work in the business and live in residential communities the indulgence of this consumer mentality is restricted to some extent by having relatively little personal money and personal space. People just cannot afford so many gadgets, so whether or not we are especially interested in environmental issues our chosen lifestyle almost enforces a reduction in harm done to the environment.

Our simple lifestyle aligns with the positive rendering of the third precept: 'With stillness, simplicity, and contentment, I purify my body.' So not only are we saving money and resources; our simple life also has a spiritual dimension. Living in a residential community helps us to live simply, to deepen spiritual friendships, and to pursue all aspects of the Buddhist life.

19

KNOW THYSELF

MANY PEOPLE have fear and suspicion about working within an institution: will they stop thinking for themselves? This could particularly be the case with an institution such as Windhorse: evolution in which so many aspects of our lives are shared. Will we just sink into group values, lose our individuality, or even become brainwashed?

Perhaps we need a definition of true individuality. I would define it as being self-aware, self-confident, empathetic, responsible, communicative, and receptive. It means having a degree of self-consciousness in which sensitivity and positivity thrive and in which one can think things through for oneself. This is quite a tall order, and requires a lot of work. Can we develop this sort of individuality in a work situation, particularly within a structured and collective institution?

It is through developing awareness of ourselves that we can become more individual. As the process of becoming an individual is long and often difficult, remembering to work deliberately to overcome such dangers is no bad thing. Our greatest ally is the fact that we do not have a fixed and unchanging self; indeed, it is because we have a changing self that we can grow and develop. It is really quite heart-warming, not to say inspiring, how people become more and more themselves, and more and more individual, as they become more mindful and aware.

I have seen many men and women coming to work for a while in one of our shops or at our warehouse and offices in Cambridge. They come, as I did, with all sorts of ideas about team-based Right Livelihood, and of 'rights', and 'wrongs'. We have assumptions that are entrenched in our being, often ones that come with our parental and social conditioning, or as a reaction to that conditioning. Some of these views may be helpful, others less so. Some of them we may know about, others we aren't even aware that we hold. Our views can gradually become more individual as we listen to our inner self – through things like meditation and study – and test our views and assumptions in discussion, and generally be open with people. It is a great joy to watch people becoming more and more themselves as they begin to think and act more freely.

Although the ideals of the business oppose the use of coercion, either subtle or gross, that denies the development of individuality, that in itself is no guarantee of success – many organizations have had fine ideals which they don't live up to. And at Windhorse:evolution we of course fall short of our ideals time and again. There have been times when probably all of us who work in the business have fallen prey to not taking real responsibility for ourselves, let alone for others, when laziness or apathy, lack of confidence or courage, are stronger than our desire for growth and change. We can sometimes be bossy or pushy for our own ends, rather than taking full account of others. At other times, the task in hand has taken precedence over what might be best for a particular individual for a longer time than is really healthy. The balance between the needs of the task, the team, and the individual is a delicate one, and needs careful attention, as it is easy to get it wrong. Any organization or institution is only as good as the people who are part of it, and these people are in constant flux. So we might find that one team in the business is going very well and exemplifying practice while another is struggling.

Perhaps the key question is: what are the practices that counter conformism or loss of individuality? The primary safeguard against this in any gross way is the practice of awareness – and its encouragement and exemplification within the institution. One aspect of this is creativity – in its broad sense of a creative approach to life. There are two ways in which the mind can function: we can act reactively, or we can act creatively. To react means essentially to be passive and respond automatically to whatever stimuli present themselves, repeating the same old patterns in the same habitual ways. Creative action, on the other hand, means responding afresh to bring into existence something that wasn't there before, be it a higher state of consciousness, a deep communication, or a work of art. Whereas the former is mechanical, the latter is spontaneous. Any creative and ethical action, which takes us beyond just an impulsive reaction, helps us to break our reactive prison of stimulus and response.

> **To react means essentially to be passive.**

The way to be creative is to look at our mental states and attempt to restrain ourselves from merely reacting to the next stimulus. Restraint alone, however, is not enough. We then need to go on to cultivate new and more skilful behaviour, otherwise we can easily slip back and find ourselves going round in the same old grooves. If we can cultivate new behaviour, we will see results; we will have been creative and therefore more individual.

Even within the reactive mind, we all have our particular biases. Some people tend to be conformist: just going along with what others say and think without testing the efficacy of what they are doing. Others can be biased towards the doggedly individualistic, veering away from any situation in which they cannot have dominance. Being individualistic might mean you have emancipated yourself from the group through your rational thinking, but emotionally you are still very caught up with it through you fight against it. Neither of these is liberated, and we probably tend to swing from one extreme to the other.

As Buddhists, we are aiming to transcend both poles and become more and more individual. To do this, we need to be able to see ourselves objectively, to understand our real motivations for doing things, and to be clear about our ideas and our ideals. Scrupulous honesty is essential in order to respond creatively to whatever life presents. It is my belief and experience that rubbing shoulders with others in a fairly intensive situation, alongside an inner journey of meditation and reflection, helps us to challenge our motivations and ideas.

Katannuta is a woman of great determination who has battled hard and honestly with herself to be creative with the tendencies towards following and merging with the group, on the one hand, and over-defensive individualism on the other. Her desire as a Buddhist is to become a true individual: a whole and integrated person, aware of and in full communication with others. I introduced Katannuta in Chapter 6 when I used the discussion between her and Satyagandhi as an example of truthful communication. I now want to follow Katannuta's progress more broadly as she takes up the path of Buddhism and explores themes of individuality within her practice.

Several years ago Katannuta lived in Sheffield, where she worked as a psychotherapist. This was a path of practice that she felt had taken her further than the political activism she had previously been strongly engaged with. However, for some reason, she wanted to learn to meditate. She taught herself from books and from bits she picked up from friends. It was a mix and match job because she didn't want to ask someone to teach her one to one.

'I depended on a view of myself as competent and capable, and somehow the prospect of asking someone to teach me something felt too exposing. My tactic was to try to know everything already, which of course put me in many difficult spots, but I could learn quickly, so I got over such difficulties with a bit of a patch job and some bluff. Showing that I wanted or needed anything, or that I didn't know about something, made me feel vulnerable as I didn't trust others' intentions very far. Most of this was pretty unconscious at the time of course, and I wouldn't have seen it in those terms then. I was putting myself in a difficult position because I couldn't let myself be taught. Being in a "lower" position in relation to someone was not something I could acknowledge comfortably. So instead I just muddled along for a couple of years with *my* sort of meditation.

'Then a friend, Carolyn, decided she wanted to learn to meditate. She went off to be taught on a beginners' introductory retreat and quickly got involved with Buddhism and the FWBO. So it was she who taught me the mindfulness of breathing and the development of loving-kindness meditations. I knew her well so I was reasonably happy for her to teach me, though she had to be delicate for it to work.'

Over the next eighteen months Katannuta continued meditating. She plied Carolyn with questions, 'What does Buddhism say about …? And what about …?' but just relying on her friend. Katannuta realized that something intangible was not being met within her therapy work and that her meditation was not what it could be, but she still had a dislike of teachers and groups.

'It's rather like the difference between going into a little shop and expecting to be served by an assistant, or going into a supermarket. I preferred the neutrality of the supermarket. I always wanted to be independent because that felt safer, despite seeing the benefits to Carolyn through the contact she was getting. I was, however, getting some of those benefits by proxy. We did lots of talking, about both meditation and Buddhism, and she was incredibly kind and patient with me. Then she made a commitment and declared she was a Buddhist and after some thought she asked me if I would like to attend the small ceremony that was to be held to mark this commitment. She didn't want to invite me if I was going to sit in a corner being critical and argumentative, but she wanted to share this significant event with me. It was quite an eye-opener for me that she had to think about whether I could be there without spoiling it for her. It made me begin to see myself in a new light.'

Once Katannuta crossed the threshold of the Buddhist Centre for this ceremony it was easier to go again. 'I started going to introductory courses and for the next couple of years I argued my way through various classes on Buddhism. There was a guy there like me who also had to keep asking questions, had to keep digging away. It wasn't very comfortable being always full of doubts and criticisms and asking questions about them – so it was good to have someone else there who needed to keep asking too. What impressed me was how I was encouraged by the class leaders to keep on questioning. There were others at the classes who were much more straightforward, simply interested and enthusiastic. But I was just encouraged to keep asking questions more fully and to keep really looking for answers, which gave me a lead into observing how my questioning was mostly just an habitual and defensive pattern. Ironically, the people I was interrogating were taking the questions much more seriously than I was taking them, which helped me to see that if they were important questions then I should follow them through, but if not, I should drop them.'

She was concerned about whether she was being sucked into a cult. She was changing so much from her contact with Buddhism that she sometimes wondered whether she was just losing her individuality, her capacity to think for herself, and her much cherished independence. She kept asking herself, 'Are these people real people? Are they able to be themselves? Are they exploring the truth or merely imbibing a doctrine?'

'These were genuine concerns for me which I took along to the classes. What I experienced was that we were a mixed bag – some of us were there for better reasons than others. But it did seem to me that the most committed people were there for the least dodgy reasons – so that was good!'

After a period of travel and then unemployment, she found herself at a crossroads: she was offered a place on a training course for the unemployed, which at the time seemed ideal.

'It was a course that would teach me to become a trainer in outdoor pursuits. It was exactly what I wanted and seemed tailor-made for me. But within half an hour of being there I knew I couldn't do it. I realized I needed something else, something much deeper. I realized that what was most important for me was the people and why they were doing what they were doing, not what they were doing. They were nice enough people on the course but I saw that what I really needed was to be with people who would help me to deepen my practice as a Buddhist. It was so quick, suddenly seeing the difference between what I felt I wanted – this course, my flat, staying in Sheffield where I felt settled and could be near the moorland – and what I found I needed: the chance to live in a spiritual community and to work with other Buddhists. I saw that what I needed was so much more than what I wanted. So I waved goodbye to the glorious north.

'There were various places in the FWBO I considered, but Carolyn helped me to see that I needed a big situation with lots of potential for friendship. At a retreat centre I might just be living and working with eight or ten people, but at Windhorse there might be a hundred others, among whom I should have a better chance of making friends.

'I had to do a lot of thinking about the ethics of working in a giftware business. When I first heard about Evolution I thought it was completely and irredeemably unethical. I couldn't see any way in which as a Buddhist you could be involved in a business that encouraged people to consume. By the time I came to ask about going to work in the accounts team, I could see that my thinking had been very black and white, indeed rather simplistic, but I still wasn't completely comfortable. When Vijayamala asked me why I wanted to work in the accounts team rather than in the shop I had to say that I hated gift shops. And she had to point out that "if you work in the accounts team you are still part of a gift business you know." At that time I would have preferred it if Windhorse had been engaged in an area that was ethically less complex – but I came to feel that the positive contribution to the world outweighed the compromises involved. I even came to see that there could be some ethical advantages in being Buddhists doing business in giftware. We want to make big profits so that we can give money away to help spread the Dharma. Trying to do that through, say, providing hospice services would be very difficult. As I say, it's a very complex area and I'm not for a moment advocating the view that the goal of bigger profits can excuse any or all behaviour. Yet gradually I came to feel that I could, in all integrity, get involved in Windhorse.'

So with encouragement from others Katannuta went to Cambridge for a three-month trial period. 'I was quite clear I was putting the accounts team on trial as much as they were.' By the time she was half way through the three months she decided it was good enough. Previously, she had always tried to find the perfect thing, which of course paralysed decision making.

'I was absolutely exhausted a lot of the time for the first few months. I was taking in so much information and dealing with feeling new, but compared to living in a flat alone and being unhappily unemployed it was heaven. I was surrounded by all these people who were busily practising away in the context of a large Buddhist centre and that was brilliant. I did find the flatlands surrounding the smug little town of Cambridge appalling. It was hard being away from the hills, so on occasion I'd borrow a company car and drive out into the countryside and lie down on the ground.... Yet the process I'd gone through to come here had worn away most of my delusions that Sheffield would still work for me as an alternative.'

The first year was hard, mainly because it was not easy to make friends despite being among so many people. Nobody had known her long, so she experienced a shallowness of communication, but there was just enough to keep her there. For three months she lived with a woman who was also new to the business, until there were a number of women needing accommodation and together they set up a community.

'There were six of us who hardly knew each other. No one had any experience of living in a spiritual community and there were no Order members to look to, so we just had to take responsibility for ourselves. It wasn't easy but it was good.'

Meanwhile there was lots of scope to take responsibility at work, training others, working with others, and learning lots about herself. Towards the end of her first year she was finally making firm friends, and this made it possible for her to stay, though she shied away from long-term commitment.

'I still had this deeply ingrained habit of keeping my options open, equating freedom with not having responsibilities. The prospect of committing myself felt horribly restricting, but ironically my experience of working in Windhorse was that the more I committed myself, the more freedom I had. There's a bit from a film where two brothers repeatedly compete against each other. The competition involves swimming out to sea and the rules are that the one who wins is the one who doesn't stop, and the one who stops and turns back is the loser. For years the elder brother always wins – except once. Years later he asks, "How did you manage to win that time?" and his younger brother says, "I didn't save anything for the way back."

'I realized that I was always holding something back, like keeping one hand on the handle of the back door, just in case this wasn't the right thing to be doing. But that holding back meant I wasn't being wholehearted, and that felt increasingly painfully unsatisfactory.

'I looked at others who had committed themselves to working in the business long term, and I could see their friendships here had a basis to grow on. I saw that as long as I was holding back in general, I was also holding back in my friendships. When I was eventually able to say that I wanted to stay a good length of time, I had an enormous release of energy. It was as though I'd been driving with the handbrake on and now I'd suddenly released it. I don't know how long I'll be here, but the more I put into the business and into my friendships the more effective I am, the more positive I am, and the more opened up. It all goes very much against my original ideas.'

I wondered whether there could be a danger of her feeling over-identified with Windhorse, as in her previous jobs and roles. 'It's true, I can get awfully pompous about what I'm doing, as though it's the only good thing in the world, but I don't think that really goes very deep. At heart, I'm well aware that our business is only a tiny thing in the world. I try to maintain a strong sense of the broader context, and I'm very curious about the way other Buddhists practise.

'As Windhorse gets bigger, I do think a lot about how we can each avoid the danger of becoming passive. How can we experience ourselves more as the business rather than a small cog within it? How can we keep feeling that we can take the initiative and make a difference? I also think about how we can devolve responsibility, and yet let the most experienced and spiritually developed people give us a lead, spiritually and commercially. All that sort of stuff fascinates me. I think it rests on good communication of our individual and collective vision and the many ways we are trying to put it into effect. That means that as we get bigger we have to ask ourselves what structures we need to evolve, what structures will keep us all up to date where it matters, build trust between us, encourage experimentation, and help us to learn from each other's experience. This experimentation and encouragement of individuals to take responsibility is the ethos at the heart of the business, even though we don't always get it perfect. It's what makes it right for me to be here.'

Katannuta was ordained in the autumn of 2000, her new name meaning 'she who has gratitude'. In the same year her good friend Carolyn became Tejapushpa, 'fiery flower'.

'More recently I've had contact with some of my old friends, and I've had some beautiful responses to what I am doing with my life. I'm a very different person to the one I used to be, and they have shown a lot of admiration that I am pursuing a life of meaning and wholeheartedness. It's the process of continually moving towards perfection with awareness and not giving up when things are just mediocre that's the key.'

People such as Katannuta beautifully demonstrate how as people grow in awareness they become different and more individual. But is it then the case that everyone would benefit from such conditions? Is it a universal good? I think this question over-simplifies people's different paths and needs, and takes us away from the Buddha's key teaching: the whole of the Noble Eightfold Path will be found where there are truth seekers. The Buddha taught that in order to make progress on the Path we need these eight elements in our life, but the way in which these manifest will vary from one person to another.

It seems as though it is sometimes difficult to distinguish between 'this is good' and 'this is good for me'. A fellow truth-seeker friend of mine would be only half-alive if he were not devoting most of his time to his painting. This would seem to rule out full-time engagement in Windhorse:evolution for him. Another person might have a strong vocation that they need to live out in order to feel fulfilled. Those people need to find their own ways of bringing their ideals into the full scope of their lives. Of course, there are many other examples, not so clear-cut. No institution can supply all our needs. This is one possible path of practice among many.

Many people who pass through the doors of Windhorse:evolution use their time with us to learn about work as a spiritual practice, and as an experience of an intensive period of spiritual engagement. They might then return to their own country (if they're from abroad) or move on to another situation within which to pursue their practice. This moving on is completely understandable, and the exchange of experience and input is mutually beneficial. It can, though, create its own difficulties for the business as there need to be a number of people who are commited to staying long-term, and around whom others come and go.

Satyaloka, who worked for Windhorse for eleven of its early years, moved on to the USA. He tells his own story about his struggles and achievements, and why he moved on.

'I worked in Windhorse from the summer of 1986 until the autumn of 1997. During that time, which was one of constant growth for the business, I was involved in many aspects of its operation. I started out as one of the van salesmen and learned the basics of the business that way. I found I had some talent for aesthetics and moved into creating a company image through trade show stand design and buying products abroad. It was a steep learning curve, because I had no prior experience of any of these areas. Later I moved into finding premises for our developing retail chain, negotiating leases and generally helping to oversee the expansion of the Evolution shops.

'Each of these moves evolved out of an existing need within the business, often matched with my desire to move into a new field. Over time, I found an increasing interest in the people side rather than the nuts and bolts of the business. This led me into doing training with Ruchiraketu, particularly in developing teamwork and the tie-up between work and the spiritual life. In practical terms, this involved facilitating a number of Right Livelihood team meetings. This and availability as a spiritual friend became my responsibilities in later years. Alongside these specific jobs, I was a director of the business for many years and worked with the other directors and management teams to oversee the spiritual and financial well-being of the business.

'I would characterize my time there as one of growing up psychologically and spiritually by learning to take responsibility for myself and my actions, as well as a certain amount of responsibility for others. I quite like the image of the spiritual community that Jiyu Kennet (the abbess of Throssle Hole Buddhist Abbey in Northumberland and later Shasta Abbey in California) used – that of a revolving tumbler that contains semiprecious stones and grit. The constant motion of rock against rock and the grit polishes each stone to reveal its unique beauty. There was a lot of grit to help the process along, but I also feel I had the great good fortune to tumble around with some very precious stones – a very capable, intelligent, and honest bunch of people who like me had their rough edges somewhat smoothed in the process of working together.

'Over time, I moved from an interest in the business as a business, to seeing it as essentially a means to an end – providing conditions in which people could spiritually develop. It was the bigger picture that now interested me. I worked quite hard on my competitiveness, status concerns, immature male moodiness, harshness, aggression, and lack of empathy. I made some progress in learning to be a team member and working cooperatively. I say I worked hard, but it wasn't particularly focused – more just putting myself into a project bigger than me and letting the needs of that call forth the necessary change in me.

'But that progress is also a deeply mysterious process. It doesn't happen in a linear way. The ways of the soul or heart are not the efficient straight lines of the canal, but more like the whimsical path of a meandering river. Spiritual growth and development in a human being can been likened to the organic process of growth in a plant. It takes in nutrients through the soil and with the presence of other elements, such as water and sunshine, it converts that energy into shoots and flowers that are completely different from the water and soil. The pattern of new growth cannot always be predicted. In the same way, one can give conscious attention to reducing a certain unskilful tendency, and the change, when it comes, may be seemingly unrelated to our area of conscious inhibition or encouragement. The spiritual life is not predictable, neat, and tidy.

'I will give an example that comes from a retreat context, but which manifested itself in my working life. Indeed, my experience of working in Windhorse was always an interplay of these two modes of life: the life of activity and the life of calm. I often felt that the ability to give oneself completely to work in which one believed was very helpful in engaging with the inner work of retreat, and vice versa.

'A year after my father died, I went on an extended retreat of four weeks, and wrote letters to my father as a way of resolving unfinished business, to grieve, and say thank you. I also remember connecting deeply with my teacher through reading one of his volumes of memoirs. During the retreat, I came to a more compassionate understanding of my father, what the difference was between a father and a spiritual teacher, and what it was reasonable to expect from a father and what it was not. Soon after my return to work, people began to comment on how much gentler I had become, how I was less harsh in my dealings with others, and less aggressive and critical. This shift seemed more permanent that the post-retreat glow, though it was by no means a total transformation as those who knew me in later years can testify.

'I had no perspective on the change. To me I was the same person, with the same internal experience, but to others I was markedly changed. I knew I could be aggressive and critical, but the extent that certain colleagues commented on the shift surprised me. This was a character fault I had made efforts to correct, and now, unbeknownst to me, there had been a shift. There is something essentially mysterious about the process of personal change. The Buddha referred to it as the greatest miracle.

'One of the main things I have taken away is the faith that a dedicated group of people working together for the same ends can achieve something of real substance that is greater than the sum of their individual efforts. It's the *raison d'être* in my mind for belonging to a spiritual community like the WBO. I have learnt that if you really commit yourself to a course of action, it brings something new into being.

'My decision to leave came as follows. I had been dissatisfied for a while, but trusted from experience that something would emerge either from within the situation or within me. This time the dissatisfaction settled and no movement from within or without seemed enough. I decided that I needed to move on. I had my conscious reasons all lined up, but I am not sure if they weren't just rationalizations to try and make sense of an intensely felt intuitive but inchoate need for change. I no longer felt very challenged by what I was doing. Obviously I could always grow more, develop more kindness, more clarity, and so on, but actually I was feeling somewhat stifled or cramped by the lifestyle I had created for myself. One of those rationales, which to this day I am not sure is true or not – or rather both is and is not true – was that I had done my spiritual growing up in Windhorse and, although I had matured, I still felt untested in a certain sense. This had been my project and I had identified wholeheartedly with it, but there was a sense that I was still junior to the more mature Vajraketu and Ruchiraketu. I needed to leave home and go out into the world.

'I had a plan in place for moving on – and then my brother committed suicide. This experience propelled me into leaving much earlier than I had planned. One of the messages of Graham's death was that there was no time for complacency. One has to live one's life to the full, and I felt I was living an increasingly predictable and routine Buddhist life and wanted to regain the passion and sense of adventure I had felt at the beginning of the project. I had hoped to persuade one of my friends to move with me onto the next project, but they were still finding Windhorse a supportive situation and weren't yet ready to leave. This proved to be quite a setback as without a close friend joining me I was to find myself a stranger in a strange land for some time.

'On the whole I am proud of what the business has been able to achieve, and I feel good about my contribution. When I reflect on my time there, what I miss most is the experience of harmoniously working with a group of capable people as a team, to make things happen. Over and above that, I miss the friends I made. On the other hand it was not all sweetness and light, and there are many things that I am glad to have left behind in the lifestyle and many unexpected gifts in my new way of living, but that is another story for another time.'

After he left, Satyaloka first went to teach at the FWBO centre in San Francisco, then moved to Missoula where he now lives with his partner. He is very active in all aspects of the local Buddhist centre and is increasingly involved in hospice work.

I hope these stories and experiences have shown these different people's struggles, doubts, and challenges as well as their successes and joys. We need to protect our ideals and our attempts to put them into practice – to rejoice in them and not let cynicism or imperfection erode our faith in change and transformation. There is always a danger, when presenting something precious, of one-sidedness and glossing over difficulties, of talking at the most ideal level, which of course exists side by side with the fact that we find the work boring at times, we get irritated, we have niggly negative responses such as 'Why don't others do things the way I do? Why don't they work harder?' and so on.

Working in team-based Right Livelihood is not all wonderful, but if we are practising sincerely we are enabling each other to make decisions, to come up with our own solutions, and to live our own lives. I'm not living my own life if I'm doing what other people think I should be doing – or, rather, what I think they think. I see part of working together as helping each other in our spiritual practice and maintaining supportive conditions as much as possible, while recognizing that no conditions are perfect.

20

CONCLUSION: WOVEN CADENCES

IT WAS WINTER when I started writing this book. It is now summer and I haven't heard the rumbling of my central heating for many months, nor breathed the fog-filled air. What were river-flooded greens and parks when I first put pen to paper, are now sun-drenched well-mown lawns speckled with cricketers and volley-ball players. Sunbathers stretch out lazily on the grass beside families eating picnics. The homeless, no longer wrapped in blankets and sleeping bags, but stripped down to singlets, still hang out with their dogs, and still beg for money and food. Pub-goers spill out into gardens, courtyards, and down onto the banks of the Cam, laughing, cajoling, and eyeing up flimsily-dressed young women. A few remaining students relax in gaggles after their finals. Overseas language students have arrived and frequent the bars, cafés, clubs, punts, and pavements, adding a bit of southern European flavour to this historical, quintessentially English city. Some of these young men and women might even make it to the Evolution shop.

This morning I awoke at 5 a.m., greeted by shafts of sunlight playing lightly on a picture on my bedroom wall beside my shrine. It is a photograph of one of Sangharakshita's Tibetan teachers. His lower torso is swathed in maroon robes. He sits leaning forward, looking out of his window, while dappled sunbeams dance around his white hair and play on his bare arm and half-covered chest. He smiles softly. Laughter lines fan out around cheek and temple from his kindly gaze, which sometimes seems to look afar, well removed from this fleeting world. At other times his cheerful contemplation appears to be surveying things close by. His eyes speak of immense love and compassion imbued with the deepest reaches of understanding. This expression sets up a reflective mood that stays with me all day.

After a period of meditation it is still only 6.30. I decide to go for a long walk before the city rises from its slumbers and set out for Grantchester. In solitude, I traverse Jesus Green and walk up the narrow lane between the shuttered terraced houses of Portugal Place – each painted a different colour and adorned with window boxes trailing red and pink geraniums. Entering Bridge Street, I peep in the windows of Garfunkel's restaurant, the site of the first Christmas Evolution shop, imagining where exactly the breeze blocks and glass of those first trendy units would have been placed. By the Round Church, I enter St John's Street. I glance up above the store logos and admire the great variety of architectural styles: Elizabethan, Georgian, Tudor. Here, no doubt, once lived men and women of the town and men of the gown. Continuing past the classical Senate House, where rules are framed and honorary degrees still conferred, I saunter on down King's Parade.

I marvel at the lavishly embellished pinnacles above the gateway to the magnificent King's College Chapel, which took seventy years to build. 'Are you building a wall, supporting wife and family, or building a cathedral?' I might have asked its stonemasons. I realize with some surprise how no one worker would have seen that project through from beginning to

culmination. What vision, what human endeavour, it represents! And I think of the hundreds of boys whose pristine voices
have sung in the chapel choir, boys who grew up and became
men, fought and died in battle, perhaps made their mark on
humanity, and long since gone to their graves. I reflect likewise
on the lofty idealism that motivates the many men and women
who have spoken in the pages of this book, while delighting in
the playing out of that idealism in the intensely 'real' world of
Windhorse:evolution. I feel gratitude towards everyone who,
over the past twenty-three years, has given so much to this big
experiment. Through each individual's desire to seek the truth,
many have made substantial changes in their lives that decid-
edly impact on my world. Furthermore, however subtly, I believe their endeavours make their creative mark on humanity.

Once in Trumpington Street, I turn down beside Little St
Mary's Church and make a deviation into its tiny overgrown
churchyard, which has always been a favourite place of mine.
There among the rambling roses I muse that the starting point
for this book was a desire to explore what it is that many of us
have poured our lives into over a number of years. I wanted to
stand back and get a broader perspective on how Windhorse:
evolution functions as a Buddhist Right Livelihood business. I
have not been disappointed. The experience of gathering information, reflection, and articulation has gone way beyond my
expectations. Enabling others to have their voice has, on occasion, moved me to laughter as well as to tears. I am enriched by
a greater sense of the diversity of these individuals as well as
their unity.

Walking back towards the river, I pass alongside the portico of
the Garden House Hotel, where I well remember a formative
afternoon meeting in the riverside lounge with Vijayamala and
Dhiranandi. We were considering whether there might be a
way to juggle members of the women's teams in the accounts

team and the shop to enable a better spread of experience and skills. We wrote out names on scraps of paper napkin, spread them out on the coffee table, and played around with possibilities.

I continue my walk across Coe Fen and Lammas Land. There are more people about now: walking their dogs, jogging, or going to an early work-shift. Most share a greeting, such as 'hello, lovely morning', greetings that don't occur later in the day. Winding my way through Newnham, I pass by the delightful well-proportioned house that for two years housed a Buddhist community of eight women who worked in the business. The lease had to be given up when the house was needed for a university couple, who apparently found it rather pokey. Now I cross Grantchester Meadows, with fields of ripening corn on my right and flower-filled grassland running down to the river on my left.

Further down the narrow track, I see a familiar figure walking towards me, Glennys, with her dog, Mutley. Glennys often helped out in Evolution in its early days. She created stunning window displays that are still talked about seven years later. I can picture now the winged, smoking dragon made *in situ* from wire and tissue paper that hung the length of a winter solstice window, stirring its reptilian body slightly and scrutinizing customers with its marble eyes as they walked in the door. She has already been down to the river at Grantchester to watch the sunlight dancing on water. We stop for a moment and have a friendly chat, trying to determine the location and identity of a noisy bird.

At Grantchester village, I head for the Orchard tea-rooms. This charming spot of literary fame has also been the site of many Buddhist meetings. We have held at least two management meetings here in recent times when we wanted to broaden our horizons from a purely business agenda. I have often commented on what an agreeable business it would be to run the garden, and such a possibility was even one of our initial ideas for a Right Livelihood business for women in Cambridge some eleven years ago. At that time, the Orchard gardens had been closed for a number of years. We set up the Evolution shop instead.

Deserted deckchairs loll invitingly beneath apple-laden trees. I sit down, quite alone, while skylark and warbler sing duets. I ponder on what a vastly different beast Windhorse:evolution is today from its beginnings in the early 1980s. There have been times when we have had to take stock and re-evaluate what we are doing, pull in the reins, and consolidate rather than expand. At one time we were small enough for everyone to know everyone else, and for most people to be in contact with what was going on in the various parts of the business. However, an ad hoc way of disseminating information can no longer be relied upon. The area of leadership is under debate, as is the theme of consultation and the need for more transparency in decision making. We have recently expanded our management team from five to ten. Everyone across the business is being encouraged to review the aims and goals of Windhorse:evolution. As a result of feedback, smaller groups of interested parties are being set up to investigate particular areas of concern, such as environmental issues, training, and internationalism. New energy is being galvanized, and it is timely, for we are moving to a new warehouse, which marks another new – and very costly – beginning.

A few raindrops begin to fall: 'a great rain cloud rises above the world covering all things everywhere ... raining down the rain of the Dharma ... the Buddha appears in the world to pour enrichment on all parched living beings.'[15] I pull a notebook from my pocket and start to write a conclusion for this book.

'Windhorse:evolution', I write, 'has no existence separate from the people within it' (and I'm obviously not talking about its legal structures here). 'It is the people that are its heart and lifeblood. It is their collective activity, which is the Bodhisattva spirit kept alive through shared and supportive conditions, a transpersonal spirit so hard to maintain in isolation. It is a team-based Right Livelihood business that is a complete spiritual practice for many who work within it, a means encompassing each limb of the Noble Eightfold Path.

'There are many voices within these pages, a cross-section of different teams and temperaments, men and women, young and old, those new to the business and long-term participants, but there are dozens of others who have not had their individual voices heard. I am well aware that each team and every Evolution shop could write its own story and share its humanity along with its successes and failures. In no way can this book reflect the complexity. My attempts can only express the spirit as I savour it. If I have been successful in sharing some of that, I shall have achieved what I set out to do.'

It is 9 a.m. on the full-moon day of June 2002. The sun shines down from a clear azure sky. Some eighty men and women stand outside the front doors of our spanking-new chrome-silver offices and warehouse. There is a short speech announcing the name of the building, Uddiyana, a mythical Tibetan kingdom that was once a meeting point for different cultures. It has associations with the Tantric guru as well as with the intensive practice of mindfulness. Keturaja cuts the blue ribbon across the doorway to a resounding threefold celebratory shout of 'Sadhu!' In silence we enter the doorway past a three-metre standing Buddha, who looks down with a compassionate smile and holds up his right hand in the gesture of fearlessness. Each of us picks up a lighted candle from the reception desk and from there we file past bemused fitters still laying the last squares of carpet and pass through into the airy warehouse. Down between the rows of racking, already stacked high with boxes, we enter a central space. There on the concrete, marked out with salt and sand, lies a mandala. We place our candles around it, circumambulate this sacred spot, and sit down on the floor and up the aisles in the four directions. A large stupa, symbolizing Enlightenment and the path leading to it, is already being sculpted elsewhere in the warehouse and will soon rise from this spot.

Much thought and care has gone into making this utilitarian building a beautiful place. Now, on a Monday morning just after Midsummer's Day, before making our way to our desks, phones, computers, or fork-lift trucks, we dedicate our new workplace as a temple of practice.

> Here may no idle word be spoken,
> Here may no unquiet thought disturb our minds.
> To the observance of the five precepts, we dedicate this place;
> To the practice of meditation, we dedicate this place;
> To the development of wisdom, we dedicate this place;
> To the attainment of Enlightenment, we dedicate this place.
> May our mind become Buddha,
> May our thought become Dharma,
> May our communication with one another be Sangha.

The marking of a new beginning is heralded by the clashing of cymbals and beating of drums. Our individual and collective transforming work will go on, and continue to be a work in progress.

REFERENCES

1   Derrick Bell, *Ethical Ambition*, Bloomsbury, London 2002, p.12

2   Śāntideva, *Bodhicaryāvatāra* 5.13

3   Śāntarakṣita, *Tattvasaṃgraha* 3147–8

4   as told by Padmasuri in *But Little Dust*, Windhorse Publications, Birmingham 1997

5   Sangharakshita, *The Ten Pillars of Buddhism*, Windhorse Publications, Birmingham 1996, p.72

6   *Mahāparinibbāna Sutta* (*Dīgha Nikāya* 16.5.13)

7   *Dhammapada* 100

8   *Sevitabbāsevitabba Sutta, Majjhima Nikāya* 114

9   *Dhammapada* 170

10 *Dhammapada* 1

11 *Dhammapada* 2

12 *Udāna* 4.1

13 *Upaḍḍha Sutta, Saṃyutta Nikāya* XLV.2

14 B.R. Ambedkar, *Buddha and the Future of His Religion*, Bheem Patrika, Jullundur 1980, p.12

15 The Parable of the Rain Cloud, from the *Saddharma-Puṇḍarīka* or *Lotus Sūtra*

FURTHER READING

Derrick Bell, *Ethical Ambition*, Bloomsbury, London, 2002

Kulananda and Dominic Houlder, *Mindfulness and Money*, Broadway Books, New York 2002

John Lane, *Timeless Simplicity*, Green Books, Vermont, 2001

Paramananda, *Change Your Mind*, Windhorse Publications, Birmingham, 1996

Sanghadevi, *Living Together*, Windhorse Publications, Birmingham, 2003

E. F. Schumaker, *Small is Beautiful*, Vintage, London, 1993

Subhuti, *The Buddhist Vision*, Windhorse Publications, Birmingham, 2001

Tarthang Tulku, *Mastering Successful Work*, Dharma Publishing, Berkeley CA, 1994

Claude Whitmyer (ed.), *Mindfulness and Meaningful Work*, Parallax Press, Berkeley CA, 1994

INDEX

The Windhorse symbolizes the energy of the enlightened mind carrying the Three Jewels – the Buddha, the Dharma, and the Sangha – to all sentient beings.

Buddhism is one of the fastest-growing spiritual traditions in the Western world. Throughout its 2,500-year history, it has always succeeded in adapting its mode of expression to suit whatever culture it has encountered.

Windhorse Publications aims to continue this tradition as Buddhism comes to the West. Today's Westerners are heirs to the entire Buddhist tradition, free to draw instruction and inspiration from all the many schools and branches. Windhorse publishes works by authors who not only understand the Buddhist tradition but are also familiar with Western culture and the Western mind.

Manuscripts welcome. For orders and catalogues contact us through our website at www.windhorsepublications.com or at

WINDHORSE PUBLICATIONS	WINDHORSE BOOKS	WEATHERHILL INC
11 PARK ROAD	PO BOX 574	41 MONROE TURNPIKE
BIRMINGHAM	NEWTOWN	TRUMBULL
B13 8AB	NSW 2042	CT 06611
UK	AUSTRALIA	USA

Windhorse Publications is an arm of the Friends of the Western Buddhist Order, which has more than sixty centres on five continents. Through these centres, members of the Western Buddhist Order offer regular programmes of events for the general public and for more experienced students. These include meditation classes, public talks, study on Buddhist themes and texts, and 'bodywork' classes such as t'ai chi, yoga, and massage. The FWBO also runs several retreat centres and the Karuna Trust, a fund-raising charity that supports social welfare projects in the slums and villages of India.

Many FWBO centres have residential spiritual communities and ethical businesses associated with them. Arts activities are encouraged too, as is the development of strong bonds of friendship between people who share the same ideals. In this way the fwbo is developing a unique approach to Buddhism, not simply as a set of techniques, less still as an exotic cultural interest, but as a creatively directed way of life for people living in the modern world.

If you would like more information about the FWBO visit the website at www.fwbo.org or write to

LONDON BUDDHIST CENTRE   ARYALOKA
51 ROMAN ROAD   HEARTWOOD CIRCLE
LONDON   NEWMARKET
E2 0HU   NH 03857
UK   USA

ALSO FROM WINDHORSE

AKKUPA

TOUCHING THE EARTH

A BUDDHIST GUIDE TO SAVING THE PLANET

This is not just another call to recycle, a litany of destruction, or a bland spiritual homily. Environmentalist and Buddhist teacher Akuppa urges us to see beyond our selfish concerns and wake up to the fragile beauty of the world. This capacity to look beyond ourselves is a seed of heroism.

Cultivating this seed, in a thousand ordinary ways, we will find real change is possible after all.

This little book is full of practical advice and profound insight. Jonathon Porritt

128 pages
ISBN 1 899579 48 6
£6.99/$9.95/€9.95

SANGHADEVI

LIVING TOGETHER

Living Together explores the essential ingredients of community living, including friendliness, cooperation, meaningful communication, and mutual vision.

Drawing on her many years in Buddhist communities, Sanghadevi, a widely-respected Buddhist teacher, encourages those who aspire to this lifestyle to engage with the frequent challenges they will encounter and speaks from her experience of the joys of sharing.

112 pages
ISBN 1 899579 50 8
£4.99/$7.95/€7.95

BODHIPAKSA

WILDMIND

A Wildmind is as spacious as a clear blue sky, as still as a lake at dawn; such a mind is a source of richness and fulfilment. It is a mind that is free, spontaeous, and abundantly creative. It is a place we can spend the rest of our lives exploring.

This is a guidebook to that inner wilderness. Buddhist meditation teacher Bodhipaksa shows us how we can use simple meditation practices to realize the potential of our minds and hearts.

Wildmind is also an on-line meditation teaching resource at www.wildmind.org

256 pages, with photographs
ISBN 1 899579 55 9
£11.99/$18.95/€18.95

SUBHUTI

THE BUDDHIST VISION: A PATH TO FULFILMENT

What is the Buddhist Vision? Put simply, it is that all human beings can develop. Every one of us can find a way beyond the dissatisfaction and suffering of everyday life and realize our full potential. In describing three important Buddhist symbols, Subhuti shows us how.

The Wheel of Life depicts how we typically experience and respond to the world. The Spiral Path describes how we can break out of this habitual pattern. The Mandala of the Five Buddhas represents the highest spiritual qualities to which we can aspire.

232 pages with diagrams
ISBN 1 899579 36 2
£11.99/$18.95/€18.95